US of AA

US
of
AA

HOW THE TWELVE STEPS HIJACKED
THE SCIENCE OF ALCOHOLISM

JOE MILLER

CHICAGO
REVIEW
PRESS

Copyright © 2019 by Joe Miller
All rights reserved
Published by Chicago Review Press Incorporated
814 North Franklin Street
Chicago, Illinois 60610
ISBN 978-1-61373-927-3

Library of Congress Cataloging-in-Publication Data
Names: Miller, Joe, 1968– author.
Title: US of AA : how the twelve steps hijacked the science of alcoholism /
    Joe Miller.
Description: Chicago, Illinois : Chicago Review Press, [2019] | Includes
    bibliographical references and index.
Identifiers: LCCN 2018050847 (print) | LCCN 2018052969 (ebook) | ISBN
    9781613739280 (PDF edition) | ISBN 9781613739303 (EPUB edition) | ISBN
    9781613739297 (Kindle edition) | ISBN 9781613739273 (cloth edition)
Subjects: LCSH: Alcoholism—Treatment—United States.
Classification: LCC RC565.7 (ebook) | LCC RC565.7 .M55 2019 (print) | DDC
    362.292—dc23
LC record available at https://lccn.loc.gov/2018050847

Typesetting: Nord Compo

Printed in the United States of America
5 4 3 2 1

To the memory of Mervyn and Mark Minichillo

CONTENTS

PROLOGUE

WE CALL ALCOHOLISM a disease, but we treat it like a story: an alcoholic takes a drink and it's like a switch turns on inside—for years and years they drink and drink, powerless to stop or slow down, even as their lives crumble around them. But there is a way out: Alcoholics Anonymous. After alcoholics have hit rock bottom, they go to AA, where they learn that they suffer from a disease, for which the only cure is God, who alone can remove their desire to drink, deliver them from destruction, and transform them into spiritual and selfless pillars of society. It's a classic story, a twisted variant of the hero's journey, told and retold in countless memoirs, magazine and newspaper articles, movies and TV shows. We've lived it with friends and family or we know people who have, and over the years of telling and retelling, it's become an indelible truth.

I started living the story in my early twenties. I'd binged all through my teens, and then something seized me from sleep one night, as if a hand had reached through my dreams, yanked me upright, and slapped my face. In the darkness my mind cleared and fixed on a stark choice: kill myself or get help. I managed to fall back to sleep, and the next day I called the county mental health office and told the woman who answered the phone I was losing my mind. She offered an appointment two weeks out. I asked if there was any help available for me to quit drinking, and she said there's AA. I found the number in the book, called, and got the answering machine, with the time and place for a meeting that day.

The meeting was at five in the afternoon in a narrow storefront downtown. It began with the Serenity Prayer, which I'd read once in a Kurt Vonnegut book. I murmured along, eyes closed, head bowed. Then everyone looked at me and smiled. This would be a "first-step meeting," the chairperson said. By tradition, he explained, whenever someone new came in, they would go around

1

the circle, say their name and "I'm an alcoholic," and share their stories—what their drinking lives had been like, what happened to them, and what their lives were like now, without alcohol. They all said they had a disease that made them drink long beyond drinking's usefulness—a disease of the body, mind, and spirit—and they were utterly powerless against it, but they could break free with God's help and the help of one another. It's progressive, they said of this disease, not only during active use but also when in remission. They told me a story about a man who had been clean and sober for many years, but he went back out and within two days he drowned in his own vomit. His disease had kept going after he quit, so when he started back up he died right away— because, unbeknownst to him, his disease had already killed him years earlier.

As my new friends went around the circle, I could nod in agreement at least once during each of their stories. I lit a cigarette and settled back in my chair, feeling warm and safe. At the end of the night they gave me a silvery tin chip that read 24 Hours and To Thine Own Self Be True. For the next several years, I went to meetings not less than three times a week, most often more.

New people would arrive all the time. Some would stay; most wouldn't. We told each other that they weren't ready, that they needed to suffer more before they were ready for help. Alcoholics need to hit bottom, we believed, in order to become willing to work the program and turn their lives over to the care of God. And some, we knew, never would. By AA's own accounting, 95 percent of the people who come to their meetings looking for help are among "such unfortunates," as they say in the program; they quit within a year. Of that 5 percent who stay a year or more, about half remain members for good, achieving long-term sobriety. AA has a story to explain the dropouts, too. They haven't suffered enough, haven't hit a low enough bottom to make them willing to embrace the cure. They just need to drink more until their life is so horrible that they're ready to "trudge the road to happy destiny." And even then, many will never be ready, will remain forever incurable. In the words of a passage that's read at the beginning of every AA meeting:

> They cannot or will not completely give themselves to this simple program, usually men and women who are constitutionally incapable of being honest with themselves. There are such unfortunates. They are not at fault; they seem to have been born that way. They are

naturally incapable of grasping and developing a manner of living which demands rigorous honesty.

I wasn't going to be one of those people. I took on a sponsor, a corporate headhunter named David, a Big Book thumper—an AA fundamentalist, one who believes that the solution to alcoholics' every problem can be found in the first 164 pages of the Big Book, AA's basic text. We met for coffee, and he showed me how to do a fourth step, following the instructions from the Big Book exactly. I wrote down every resentment I'd ever had against anyone, and then I went about figuring out where I was at fault in each situation. What it boiled down to was four character defects: selfishness, self-seeking, dishonesty, and fear. I worked on it every day, several times a day, and as I wrote I felt a kind of energy flow into me, not necessarily from what was going down on the page—the words were so repetitive it was like being a kid forced to write self-admonishments over and over on a chalkboard—but because I was being active in my recovery, I was doing something to make myself better, and that felt good.

When I was done, I met with David and together we went through the fifth step: "Admitted to God, to ourselves, and to another human being the exact nature of our wrongs." It took all of twenty minutes.

The Big Book promises:

> Once we have taken this step, withholding nothing, we are delighted. We can look the world in the eye. We can be alone at perfect peace and ease. Our fears fall from us. We begin to feel the nearness of our Creator. We may have had certain spiritual beliefs, but now we begin to have a spiritual experience. The feeling that the drink problem has disappeared will often come strongly. We feel we are on the Broad Highway, walking hand in hand with the Spirit of the Universe.

But these feelings eluded me. When I finished the fifth step I felt a sense of accomplishment, but inside I was the same old me. In my journal that night I wrote a long, resentful screed against my roommate.

I graduated from college and drifted away from my college AA group. I landed a job at the local alternative weekly newspaper, a place where drinking was part of the culture. On Tuesday nights, as we worked late putting the paper to bed, my coworkers would make a beer run, and everyone would work with an open bottle next to the keyboard, everyone but me. I wanted one too, and I began to think that maybe I wasn't an alcoholic, that perhaps the problem that led me to AA years earlier was youth and immaturity. One night I had my coworkers over for a party at my apartment. They shoved their six-packs into the fridge next to my cans of sparkling water, and when the evening was done there were a few beers left. I thought about them all night and well into the next day. I took one out and popped it open. It was a local microbrew, a nut brown ale, and it felt good to sip it as I sat in the warm autumn sun. I went back to the fridge and had another.

In time I fell back into daily drinking. And after four years I found myself in a strange new city with no friends, drinking to stumbling spins every night. I'd wake up so down that I had to clench every fiber of body and soul just to make it to and through work. I went to a psychologist for help and he yelled at me, said I needed to go to AA. I went to my psychiatrist and asked for a prescription for the alcohol treatment drug Antabuse (disulfiram) and he refused, told me to go to AA.

I found an AA club a block away from my apartment and, believing there was no other solution, I started going to meetings there every day.

There's a saying that the definition of insanity is doing the same thing over and over and expecting different results. In AA it refers to drinking, of course, but it can also be applied to AA itself. I started working with a sponsor again, and when he told me I'd have to do another by-the-Big-Book fourth step, I got a new sponsor. When that sponsor said the same thing, I decided to forgo the whole sponsor thing altogether and just, as they say, don't drink and go to meetings. The meetings were insufferable. It was all the same conversation we were having when I was in my early twenties, when I still believed it contained the answers to life. But now I didn't, and every minute I sat listening felt like an hour of penance. I'd smoke cigarettes and watch the clock, and I would leave the second we'd say amen.

Unbeknownst to me, there were other options available. In the mid-1990s, right around the time I relapsed, the FDA had approved a medicine—naltrexone—for use in the treatment of alcoholism, after years of studies had shown that it reduced alcohol cravings for some alcoholics and helped them to reduce or quit their drinking. There were also alternative mutual-help groups, such as SMART Recovery and Moderation Management, which offer pathways to treatment based in the cognitive behavioral psychology principles that have withstood years of scientific scrutiny.

AA, on the other hand, defies scientific study. The 95 percent failure rate, for instance, comes from AA's own annual surveys, which are not even remotely scientific. They're conducted on a volunteer basis, anonymously. The best they can do is give a sense of the demographics of a typical AA meeting: two-thirds men, almost 90 percent white, mostly ages thirty to sixty, average sobriety of ten years. True scientific scrutiny of AA's effectiveness is nearly impossible. As an all-volunteer organization that holds as one of its most important principles the anonymity of its members, AA defies scientific standards of precise measurement—randomized trials with a control group and long-term follow-up.

Scientists have tried, but the results have been far from satisfying. In 2006, a trio of Italian scientists working with the Cochrane Collaboration, an independent worldwide network of doctors and researchers, published a meta-analysis, a review of all the randomized controlled trials ever conducted to compare AA to other forms of treatment and to no treatment at all. They scoured the scientific record for studies that fit their criteria, forty years' worth of research, and they found just eight, involving a total of 3,417 problem drinkers. In the end they ran the numbers and decided that "the available experimental studies did not demonstrate the effectiveness of AA or other twelve-step approaches in reducing alcohol use."

Out of fifty treatment methods ranked by the strength of the scientific evidence for each one's effectiveness, AA comes in thirty-eighth, according to research conducted by Dr. William R. Miller, emeritus distinguished professor of psychology and psychiatry at the University of New Mexico's Center on Alcoholism, Substance Abuse, and Addictions. In Miller's rankings, AA is below cognitive behavioral therapy and aversion therapy and regular therapy, below marriage counseling and self-help books, naltrexone, and another FDA-approved drug called acamprosate, below psychedelic drugs and even placebos.

An estimated seventeen million Americans suffer from drinking disorders, which kill nearly ninety thousand people in the United States every year, making it the nation's third leading cause of preventable death. But most of these problem drinkers don't seek or receive any treatment for their ailment—more than two-thirds of them, according to a national epidemiological study published in 2007 by the *Archives of General Psychiatry*. There are medications available that have been proven to help some alcoholics stop or reduce problem drinking, but fewer than one in ten problem drinkers receives prescriptions for them, according to a 2014 study in *JAMA*, the journal of the American Medical Association. People with drinking problems are typically referred to "group-based, abstinence-oriented treatment programs relying on the 12-step principles of Alcoholics Anonymous," *JAMA* wrote in explanation for the dismal numbers. "While many patients report benefit from these programs, most programs are not staffed by clinicians who can prescribe medications to treat [alcoholism] and most do not offer evidence-based behavioral treatments. Many health care professionals do not realize there are treatment options." In a scathing editorial that accompanied the report, the journal declared that alcoholics "receive poorer-quality care than patients with any other common chronic condition."

This is, of course, a story, too. For almost as long as AA has been in existence, scientists have argued about whether or not alcoholism is in fact the kind of disease that's described at AA meetings, and to this day there is no consensus about it. One top scientist at Brown University told me he sees it as "a learned behavior," while one of his former students—now a director of a research division in the National Institute on Alcohol Abuse and Alcoholism (NIAAA)—emphatically insisted it's a disease. When I later shared this disagreement with Dr. George Koob, director of the NIAAA, he said, "It's both."

Indeed, officials at the NIAAA prefer to avoid the word *alcoholism*, despite its presence in the very name of the institute. Instead, they use the term "alcohol use disorder," or AUD, and the scientific community generally does as well. This phrase better encompasses the full range of people who struggle with alcohol problems—from chronic conditions to acute ones—for whom AA is but one remedy among many. In the words of Marsha Vannicelli, a psychologist who specializes in treating addictions, "It's great for people it's great for, and not great for people it's not."

Yet AA is, for all intents and purposes, America's de facto policy for treating alcoholism. This book tells the story of how this came to be. Over the years, there have been a number of books about the many shortcomings of AA as a treatment policy, most notably and recently *The Sober Truth: Debunking the Bad Science Behind 12-Step Programs and the Rehab Industry*, by Dr. Lance Dodes. These books have been well researched and filled with irrefutable facts.

But when held up against the anecdotal evidence surrounding AA—the many compelling stories of people who have turned their lives around with the help of the Twelve Steps—they can come across as anti-AA polemics and are subsequently ignored or dismissed. By instead framing this science in its own history, by focusing on the people who drove it forward and drawing them out as characters, highlighting the drama of their triumphs and setbacks across a series of events that actually happened, this book hews to the old adage of "showing, not telling," and presents the science in a way that's more tangible and difficult to deny.

This story is a distinctly American one. It begins in the early years after Prohibition, and it's shaped in part by the same religious convictions that led to that failed "noble experiment" in the first place. What's baffling about the story, however, is science's complicity in writing it. Despite the dearth of scientific support for the concept of alcoholism as a disease that lies at the center of AA's remedy, science plays a key role in the story. But it's not the kind of science story we've come to know and trust, not the ever-upward-and-onward tale of discovery and innovation, of unbiased, fact-hungry truth. This story follows the same plotline as alcoholism, from the seduction of the easy fix, through the delusional halcyon days, and down and down till our hero—science—finds herself and builds her life anew.

1 | 1934–1944: BIRTH OF A DISEASE

The Little Doctor Who Loved Drunks

The earliest American notion of heavy drinking as an illness appeared in 1805, when Benjamin Rush, a preeminent American doctor of the Revolutionary War era and one of the signers of the Declaration of Independence, took quill to parchment and authored a pamphlet, "Inquiry into the Effects of Ardent Spirits upon the Human Body and Mind," in which he argued that "habitual drunkenness should be regarded not as a bad habit but as a disease," that it's "a palsy of the will," an "odious disease (for by that name it should be called)." He enumerated more than a dozen symptoms, from "unusual garrulity" to "unusual silence" to "certain extravagant acts which indicate a temporary fit of madness" such as "singing, balling, roaring, imitating the noises of brute animals, jumping, tearing off clothes, dancing naked, breaking glasses and china, and dashing other articles of household furniture upon the ground, or floor."

Rush believed "drunkenness" to be a progressive disease, much the way proponents of AA do today. "Its paroxysms occur," he wrote, "like the paroxysms of many diseases, at certain periods, and after longer or shorter intervals. They often begin with annual, and gradually increase in their frequency, until they appear in quarterly, monthly, weekly, and quotidian, or daily periods. Finally, they afford scarcely any marks of remission either during the day or the night." He even speculated as to its hereditary nature: "I have once known it to descend from a father to four out of his five children."

9

It wasn't until nearly fifty years later that Rush's malady got a proper name. In 1852, Swedish physician Magus Huss coined the term "alcoholism" in his book *Alcoholismus Chronicus*. And even then it didn't take hold in the lexicon of medicine, much less popular society. Through the nineteenth century and into the twentieth, excessive drinking was seen primarily as an issue of character or as an inevitable result of the destructive force of a terrible drug. Throughout the 1800s there appeared in the United States a smattering of sanitariums to help heavy drinkers find their way to sobriety, but the bulk of the energy against drunkenness was channeled through the temperance movement toward outlawing alcohol. People looked down on drunkards as degenerates, weak-willed and depraved.

The conception of alcoholism that's commonly held today, the one proliferated by AA, can be traced back to the early twentieth century and an otherwise undistinguished doctor named William Silkworth. Known affectionately in AA lore as "the little doctor who loved drunks," he had a solid education, having graduated from Princeton in 1896 and receiving his medical degree from NYU in 1900. He did his intern work at Bellevue Hospital in New York, where he found himself gravitating toward the drunk wards. A slight man with a gaunt face, ghostly white skin and hair, and piercing blue eyes, his diminutive, ethereal appearance was said to have put alcoholics at ease. Silkworth saw in drunks redeeming qualities that others couldn't see, a human frailness that evoked his sympathies and curiosity. He spent more and more time with them, talking, asking questions, getting to know them, puzzling over what made them drink so. When a burly man in the throes of withdrawal dropped to his knees, crying, and begged for a drink, a story began to emerge in Silkworth's mind. "I said to myself then and there," he would later recall, "this is not just a vice or habit. This is compulsion, this is pathological craving, this is disease."

Alcoholism was not a common interest among doctors at the time. There were almost no opportunities for a doctor such as Silkworth with an interest in helping problem drinkers. Most hospitals wouldn't accept alcoholics. By and large the only ones that would were state hospitals, what people at the time would've referred to as "the loony bin." In New York, however, there was one: Charles B. Towns Hospital, a private facility at 293 Central Park West. It catered to wealthy patients looking to dry out from drunken binges. Founded in the early twentieth century by its namesake, a man with no background in medicine or psychology, the hospital attracted most of its patients through advertisements in New York's many daily newspapers and through word of mouth (though legend has it that Towns was known to literally kidnap drunks and force his treatment on them). For the price of about $350 for a five-day stay, patients were given comfortable rooms, bathrobes and slippers, and access to an elegant spa as they suffered through the "Towns-Lambert Treatment"— a two-day regimen consisting of ample hourly doses of *Atropa belladonna* (a hallucinogen more popularly known as deadly nightshade) mixed with henbane (also a deliriant), and prickly ash, to alleviate the intestinal cramps caused by the psychedelics. On top of this toxic cocktail, patients would often also experience delirium tremens (DTs), an agonizing and hallucinatory condition caused by alcohol withdrawal. Towns claimed a cure rate at 75 to 90 percent, deduced from the number of patients who tried it once and never came back.

Shortly after World War I, Silkworth took a job at Towns Hospital. Over the course of his tenure, he developed a theory that alcoholics suffer from a "phenomenon of craving" that drives them to drink at dangerous levels. The cravings are physiologically based, he believed. "Alcoholism is an allergic state," he would later write, "the result of gradually increasing sensitization by alcohol over a more or less extended period of time . . . some are allergic from birth, but the condition usually develops later in life. The development and course of these cases are quite comparable with the history of hay fever patients."

Silkworth was not a distinguished or reputable researcher. He wrote only a few papers in his career, one of which was "Alcoholism as a Manifestation of Allergy," quoted above and published in 1937. In it he added that his findings were based on "observation of numerous cases at Towns Hospital, New York City, over a period of years, clinical constants have been derived and data have been accumulated"—a vague set of parameters within which to place his claims. It offers virtually no hard data or clinical observations but instead lays out the outlines of a story. An alcoholic "cannot take his liquor or leave it," he opined. "The phenomenon of craving is prominent; there are complete loss of appetite, insomnia, dry skin and hypermotor activity. He has a feeling of anxiety which amounts to a nameless terror." This inevitably draws the alcoholic to another drink, which only makes the condition worse. What's more, alcoholics can never rid themselves of their malady. "It is noteworthy that such patients may be deprived of liquor altogether for a long period, a year or longer for example, and become apparently normal," Silkworth observed. "They are still allergic, however, and a single drink will develop the full symptomatology again."

This article received no attention in the scientific community except for an article refuting it, written by a top physiologist at Yale. "The concept of an allergic reaction to alcohol has had little scientific support," wrote Dr. Howard Haggard, and "is supported only by analogy, metaphor and connotation. It is an expression, and unfortunately an erroneous one, of the long and disappointing search for a cellular basis for craving for and habituation to alcohol." He warned that "the acceptance of an erroneous explanation, whatever its originally intended purpose, may be more detrimental to progress than is ignorance. It tends to stop progress."

Nonetheless, Silkworth operated under this theory for decades without receiving any attention or exerting any influence on the medical field. He wasn't an active member of any professional association, nor was he affiliated with an academic institution, and the few articles he published in medical journals were largely ignored by their intended audience. It's likely he would have died in obscurity if he hadn't treated one fateful alcoholic who sought treatment at Towns several times in 1934 and 1935: Bill Wilson, who would go on to be cofounder of Alcoholics Anonymous.

A Flash of Light

Of all the stories in the annals of alcoholism, perhaps the most harrowing is that of William Wilson, better known as Bill W., cofounder of Alcoholics Anonymous. Throughout Prohibition, he drank "'Bathtub' gin, two bottles a day, and often three," he wrote in a short memoir that serves as the first chapter of his book *Alcoholics Anonymous*. (It's this text that's now better known as the Big Book.) He'd quit from time to time, sometimes staying sober for weeks or a month or more, but he would eventually always swing back around to having a drink, and then another, and dozens more.

He was unemployed, living on his wife Lois's meager draw as a department store clerk. In 1934, his brother-in-law footed the bill for him to take the treatment at Towns Hospital, where he came under the care of Dr. Silkworth, who told him that he suffered from a kind of allergy that caused him to react differently to alcohol than most people, that booze triggered a physiological impulse to drink and drink and drink. The story resonated with Wilson. He felt a kind of relief—he wasn't weak-willed and immoral, he was sick, biologically incapable of controlling his drinking. He just had to stay away from that first drink. And for a few months, he did so—the knowledge of his condition kept him sober. But then one day he had a drink, and suddenly he was back to drinking around the clock. His wife Lois consulted with Silkworth, who told her that he was a "hopeless" drunk and that it was likely he'd never get well. He warned that she would likely have to commit him to an asylum in order to save his life.

If Wilson were to have any hope of quitting drinking, his story needed another plotline, a third-act twist. It came from an unexpected place. Out of the blue one day he received a visit from an old drinking buddy, a man named Ebby whose drinking had been even worse than his. It cheered him; at least for one day he wouldn't have to drink alone. He offered his friend a tumbler of gin and lemonade. His friend shook his head.

Wilson, incredulous, asked his friend what had happened to him.

The friend smiled and said, "I've got religion."

"I was aghast," Wilson would later write, and he poured himself a tall drink, bracing for the sermon he was sure would follow.

But his friend didn't preach. He just told his story, how a mutual friend of theirs named Rowland had traveled to Switzerland to be treated for his alcoholism by the great psychologist Dr. Carl Jung, who hadn't offered a psychological cure but instead said the only hope for hopeless alcoholics such as he was to somehow have "a spiritual experience." Rowland sought this through a religious movement of the time called the Oxford Group. It had emerged between the world wars, and it was modeled on first-century Christianity. All the problems on Earth, they believed, are caused by people's own selfishness and fear. The world is insane and the only way to be sane in it is to surrender completely to "God-Control." The group offered a multistep process through which to achieve sanity, one of which was to bring new followers to the group. They aimed for high-profile members, and among their recruits were Harry Truman, Mae West, Joe DiMaggio, and Henry Ford; but they also sought regular folks and people who were struggling spiritually, such as heavy drinkers. Rowland had evangelized to Ebby, and now Ebby was doing the same to Wilson.

Wilson, an avowed atheist, recoiled at the notion that God could save him. Ebby asked him, "Why don't you choose your own conception of God?" The idea intrigued Wilson, stuck with him, and he started attending Oxford Group meetings in New York. It didn't much work—he continued to drink night and day, and he would show up at meetings in a stupor. He wound up back at Towns Hospital, back in Silkworth's care.

Once again under the influence of belladonna, he felt himself falling into a deep, deep depression. His life seemed worthless, with no purpose and no prospect other than the continued misery of drinking until its fast-approaching end in an insane asylum or with suicide or liver disease. He was at absolute rock bottom. Consumed with despair, he fell to his knees and cried out to God. Then, all at once, a flash of light consumed him and his body seemed to fill with a cleansing wind. Immediately his desire to drink disappeared, and it didn't return the next day when he woke up. Indeed, he felt better than he had in years.

He asked Silkworth if he was going insane.

"No, Bill, you are not crazy," the doctor said. "There has been some basic psychological or spiritual event here. Whatever you've got now, you better hold onto. It's so much better than what you had only a couple hours ago."

"He Hasn't Suffered Enough"

And so began what would become America's modern alcoholism treatment system, with a discredited scientific theory and a startling hallucination. It was a tenuous beginning. Wilson was sober, but he had no job, was living week to week off of Lois's paltry department store paycheck, and he was depressed. "I was not too well at the time, and was plagued with waves of self-pity and resentment," he would later write. "This sometimes nearly drove me back to drink, but I soon found that when all other measures failed, work with another alcoholic would save the day."

He'd visit and revisit Towns Hospital looking for drunks who might be ready to quit, hoping he might help them the way his old friend Ebby had. He'd tell them about the spiritual experience he'd had at Towns Hospital, how it had delivered him from his desire to drink. It was the only thing that seemed to lift him from his depression. But while it helped him, it never worked for the people he was trying to help. He couldn't get any of his prospects to quit drinking, much less attend an Oxford Group meeting with him.

"For God's sake stop preaching," Dr. Silkworth scolded him. "You're scaring the poor drunks half crazy. They want to get sober, but you're telling them they can only do it as you did, with some special hot flash." The doctor said to instead "give them the hard medical facts. Tell about the hopeless condition, a matter of life and death." There were, of course, no such hard medical facts, but Silkworth urged Wilson to sell them on the story of alcoholism, that they suffer from an allergy, a disease that they have no control over that compels them to drink themselves to death.

"You've got to deflate these people first. So give them the medical business, and give it to them hard," he said. "Pour it right into them about the obsession that condemns them to drink and the physical sensitivity or allergy of the body that condemns them to go mad or die if they keep on drinking."

Wilson landed a temporary job that took him away from New York for a while. A Wall Street firm was trying to take over a small machine tool company in Akron, Ohio, and it hired Wilson to go out and serve as its proxy. Five months sober, he took a train to the Midwest and checked in at the Mayflower Hotel. His task, he quickly learned, was nearly impossible; the company's local leadership was dug in, and the deliberations were acrimonious. Wilson grew depressed and lonely, with too much time on his hands. One afternoon he was in the sleek art deco lobby of the Mayflower, listening to the sound of laughter coming from the bar. He ached for the camaraderie he'd find there, for the calming buzz of a stiff drink.

The thought terrified him. One drink, he knew, would lead to another and another and he'd be plastered again, back to his old misery. He needed to find another alcoholic to talk to, someone he could try to help, so as to help himself.

In a corner of the lobby was a public phone and a church directory. He sat down and dialed a number at random. A preacher answered, and Wilson told his story, that he was an alcoholic from New York who hadn't had a drink in months, but he needed to help another alcoholic in order to stay sober. The preacher seemed to understand, and he offered a list of ten people. Wilson dialed down the list with no luck until he got to the last number. A woman answered, and after hearing Wilson's spiel, she said she had just the right person for him—a doctor who had once enjoyed a sterling reputation in Akron but had fallen so deep into his drinking that his practice was all but ruined. The woman arranged for Wilson to meet the doctor the next day.

The doctor was a proctologist named Robert Smith. At first he had wanted nothing to do with anybody who wanted to help him stop drinking. He'd already tried everything—the Oxford Group, psychology, every quack "cure" that was going around—and nothing had worked. Dozens of people had lectured him, pleaded with him, and prayed for him, and he was tired of listening. But this visitor claimed that he needed to talk to him to help himself, said it would keep him sober to meet with another drunk, so Smith agreed, thinking he was doing the poor man a favor.

When Wilson arrived at Smith's house late in the afternoon the next day, Smith's wife brewed them a pot of coffee. Wilson had come determined to heed Dr. Silkworth's advice, to lean heavily into the story of alcoholism as an ailment, to "give the hard medical facts," as Silkworth had coached him. He started off telling of his own journey through alcoholism, the anguish of drinking day in and day out and the maddening inability to stop or even slow down, and he peppered it with pithy quotes from Silkworth about the physiological nature of his struggle. Smith listened intently, fascinated by what he was hearing. Despite his medical training, he'd given little consideration to the possibility that he suffered from a physiological malady; he'd always assumed, just as most people did, his problem was an issue of morality and weakness of will.

"He was the first living human with whom I had ever talked who knew what he was talking about in regard to alcoholism from actual experience," Smith would later say of Wilson. "In other words, he talked my language."

They finished the first pot of coffee and started another. What was supposed to be a fifteen-minute meeting stretched into hours. Wilson moved into the Smiths' home and lived there for three months. They started each day with a devotion; Smith was also a member of the Oxford Group, so they shared similar sensibilities about spirituality and its power to keep them from drinking.

A few weeks into his tenuous sobriety, Smith traveled to Atlantic City to attend an American Medical Association convention, had a drink, and off he went on a bender. He returned to Akron so drunk that he called his secretary from the train station instead of his wife, but that was the last of it for him. On June 10, 1935, he began a stretch of sober days that would last the rest of his life. The date would go down in history as the day Alcoholics Anonymous was founded.

Smith and Wilson set out in search of other hard drinkers to help, so as to help themselves and to perhaps build on whatever it was they had going. They networked through churches and visited drunk wards in public hospitals. Their strategy was to "hit first with the medical facts," to describe alcoholism as a "fatal illness and that the only way a man could recover from it—or rather, not die from it—was not to take a drink to start with," according to *Dr. Bob and the Good Oldtimers*, a historical account later published by AA. They'd compare alcoholics and alcohol to diabetics and sugar and tell their own harrowing stories. Gradually they'd move into the spiritual aspects of their cure and ask their new recruits to kneel with them and pray.

The first serious candidate for their remedy was a man named Eddie who was from a prominent family in Youngstown. They worked on him for weeks. At one point, he ran off to commit suicide, but he called Smith before jumping off a bridge. He drank again. They tracked him down and locked him in the Smiths' house to keep him from drinking, but then he chased Smith's wife around with a knife.

They gave up on Eddie and went back to Akron City Hospital looking for someone else to help. A nurse there said she had "a dandy," a man named Bill, and with him the message stuck. He seized on the story Wilson and Smith were sharing as his salvation and became "AA Number Three." He's immortalized in a painting of Wilson and Smith by his hospital bedside that was made into a poster that to this day can be found adorning the walls of AA clubhouses around the world.

Bill joined them in trying to convert more drunks. They tried and failed with several more men before they converted a fourth, Ernie. But he would later relapse, too, and spend the rest of his life going back and forth between abstinence and hard drinking.

They treated their evangelism like a full-time job, spending hours sharing their story of alcoholism, praying, serving their recruits tomatoes, Karo syrup, and sauerkraut to revitalize them with vitamins. But failure was the norm rather than the exception. At the end of the summer, when it was time for Wilson to return to New York, after trying and failing to sober up dozens of drunks, there were just four members of their little group. It took another month to succeed with a fifth. Over the next year and a half, they'd manage to amass only a dozen more.

The more they tried and failed to sober others up, the more it became clear to them that suffering was an indispensable part of the cure. In order to buy into their story—especially the part about having to quit drinking and to turn everything in their lives over to a faith in God—their recruits had to have been driven to death's door.

Knowing this, they became choosy about whom they'd help. They discouraged young people from joining them—in large part because Ernie had been in his early thirties when they tried unsuccessfully to save him. As one early member named Archie would later recall, his doctor took him to see Smith. "He looked at me," Archie said of the AA cofounder. "I was only 32, and I was shaking so bad. I remember how I tried to hide my hands. 'You're pretty young,' he said. 'I don't know if you can make it.' Then he said, 'I haven't got any time or strength to waste on this unless you're serious about it.'"

The wife of another would-be new member named Clarence from Cleveland called Smith in early 1938 and, as she would recall in an AA-published history, "Right away, he wanted to know how old Clarence was. 'Thirty-four,' I said.

"'Impossible,' he replied. 'He hasn't suffered enough.'"

As with the unproven claim that alcoholism is an allergy and that its surest cure is spiritual, this belief that alcoholics have to nearly drink themselves to death before they're ready to become sober became an essential part of the alcoholism story upon which America's treatment policy would be based. This brought great danger because it serves almost as a mandate for problem drinkers to keep drinking, indeed to drink even more.

"Isn't Money Going to Spoil This Thing?"

After Wilson returned to New York, he and Lois transformed their meager apartment into a kind of makeshift treatment facility. Wilson would seek out drunks on the street or at Towns Hospital, and he and Lois would welcome them into their home. They'd hold meetings in their living room on Tuesday nights, and they'd allow two or three of the more hard-up cases to stay with them, eating their syrup, tomato, and sauerkraut concoction, listening to Wilson talk about the disease of alcoholism and the relief God could provide. Sometimes the house would become overrun; one of the new recruits would manage to sneak in a bottle of booze and the whole crowd would get roaring drunk, tearing the place up. One man committed suicide in their bathroom. More often, recruits would amass some weeks and even months of sobriety and then have a drink and go right back to their old ways. "When a member they had known for months, had had faith in, had loved, would turn up drunk, a kind of terrible apprehension would settle over the meeting," wrote Robert

Thomsen in *Bill W.*, one of several biographies of Wilson. "They'd look at one another and see the same question in each man's eyes: 'Who would be next?'"

The vast majority of their recruits failed, but amid all the setbacks there were great breakthroughs, and the number of sober members grew. One night Wilson was riding down Park Avenue with two sober members named Hank and Fitz in Hank's convertible with the top town, when Hank suddenly stood and cried out, "God almighty, booze was never this good!"

Smith was running the same kind of treatment program out of his home in Akron. Word spread, and drunks began driving down from Cleveland to attend Smith's meetings. In time they founded their own group back home. Soon there were dozens of them meeting regularly in the three cities, staying sober. Working concurrently and corresponding via letters, they developed a program of action based on the multistep process followed in the Oxford Group, which began with surrender to powerlessness, a conversion to faith in the power of God, a confession of sins, and an atonement for those sins.

Their formula for a cure was still nebulous, and it didn't work for everybody. But in 1937, two years into their improvised venture, Wilson returned to Akron, and he and Smith were sitting in the doctor's living room counting how many hopeless cases they'd turned around. All told, they estimated thirty-five or forty, out of hundreds they'd tried to save. "Bob and I saw for the first time that this thing was going to succeed," Wilson would later recall in a 1954 speech to AA members in Texas. "That God in his providence and mercy had thrown a new light into the dark caves where we and our kind had been and were still by the millions dwelling. I never can forget the elation and ecstasy that seized us both."

Wilson remained unemployed, and Smith's practice was still almost nonexistent, so the two were in rough financial shape, barely able to keep up their house payments. They didn't want regular jobs; all they wanted to do was help other alcoholics, even if there was no money in it. Then, suddenly, it seemed there might be: Charlie Towns, founder of the hospital where Wilson first got sober, reached out to Wilson with a job offer. Towns would pay Wilson to bring his fledgling alcoholism treatment program into his hospital and to serve as a lay therapist.

Thrilled at the prospect, Wilson told the fellow members of his group of his good fortune, and one by one they urged him to turn it down, saying it would professionalize whatever it was they had going and ruin it. Theirs was a program where alcoholics helped one another so as to help themselves, not to earn a paycheck. In time, what Towns was proposing would become the norm in America's treatment system, where members of AA are hired without graduate degrees but instead on the basis of their personal experience in recovery. But from the vantage point of their small, as-yet-unnamed organization of recovering alcoholics, it seemed to Wilson that his fellow members were right, and he called Towns the next day to refuse his offer.

Still, Wilson saw something big in what they were doing, an opportunity to help not just a few dozen people but hundreds of thousands, perhaps millions. He envisioned a nationwide network of treatment centers where drunks could dry out and begin working the early steps of the multistep program they were still fine-tuning. Recovering alcoholics would receive "sabbatical" stipends to allow them to take time off from their careers to serve as "evangelists" who would find alcoholics, share their stories with them, and help them find their way to recovery.

He took the idea to the group. "Almost with one voice," Wilson would recall, "they chorused, 'Let's keep it simple. This is going to bring money into this thing, this is going to create a professional class. We'll all be ruined.'"

"How in God's name are we going to carry this message to others?" Wilson replied. "We've got to take some kind of chance."

He persuaded a slim majority to back his scheme, and he set about trying to raise the money for it. Among the first people he called was his brother-in-law, a doctor, who said he knew a woman whose uncle was connected with the billionaire industrialist John D. Rockefeller Jr. Rockefeller had been a strong proponent of Prohibition, and he'd generously given to the cause. When the noble experiment proved itself a failure, he'd joined the argument for repeal, though he remained convinced that alcohol and heavy drinking posed a serious threat to American society. So he seemed an ideal candidate to fund an effort to help problem drinkers put down the bottle.

Wilson first met with Rockefeller's assistant, who agreed to take the idea to his boss, who liked what he heard. "Rockefeller was impressed," Thomsen wrote in *Bill W.* "He saw the parallel with early Christianity and along with this he spotted a combination of medicine and religion that appealed to his charitable inclination."

But, he asked, "Isn't money going to spoil this thing?"

Answering his own question, he offered $5,000 for Wilson and Smith to be able to pay their mortgages and draw $30 a week. He gave them pro bono hours with his company's lawyers. He did not give the millions Wilson was hoping for.

A Fire in the Basement

Looking back, the idea that Wilson proposed to Rockefeller is remarkably like the treatment system that would develop out of his early efforts, despite the billionaire's admonition. But it would take more than philanthropy to enable this quasi-religious, pseudoscientific program of recovery to become America's de facto alcoholism treatment policy. Larger social forces would have to align to make it so. Fortunately for Wilson and his cohorts, the social climate around the issue of alcohol in the United States was just right in the late 1930s for the incubation of their embryonic system of cure.

History portrays the end of Prohibition as instant and decisive: the noble experiment had been a resounding failure, and the nation came together as one to send it sailing into the past. But in fact, the relegalization of alcohol had not happened smoothly, and there was a very real possibility that Prohibition would be brought back. In the early years of repeal, as states scrambled to implement regulation systems, public intoxication arrests rose, and there were more drunk driving deaths than ever before, more women drinking, more kids drinking, even more bootlegging and more smuggling. Anti-alcohol "drys" were reenergized, "on the warpath again," in the words of the *Christian Century*, which was cheering them on. "If civilization survives at all," the magazine declared in 1936,

> it must be learned of men that the liquor traffic, like the slave traffic, the white slave traffic, the drug traffic, must be abolished altogether by due fiat of law, if its inherent evils, so fatal to public welfare, are to be conquered. Prohibition is the one way out—prohibition sustained, as the abolition of the slave trade was sustained through nearly a half-century of unremitting struggle, by a public opinion which refuses, through however long a time, to be defeated.

People across the country poured money into temperance groups, increasing their numbers, and leaned hard on their elected officials to bring Prohibition back. In hundreds of local elections across the country, towns and cities and counties were voting to ban liquor, taking "the first step in a scheme to have nationwide prohibition in 1945." Even the repeal-friendly *New York Times* had to concede, "It is practically a foregone conclusion that liquor will lose."

It was not the ideal climate for a scientific approach to the problem, though there were those who tried. One attempt arose from the Virginia state legislature, which sought in the first year of repeal to update its public school system's materials related to alcohol. Toward the end of the nineteenth century, as prohibition forces were growing in strength, Virginia and virtually all other states began adding to their public school curricula required lessons on alcohol. Virginia's statute, adopted in 1900, stipulated that schools "shall treat the evil effects of alcohol and other narcotics on the human system." To achieve this, the state required students to read a textbook that taught that "alcohol used as men ordinarily use it causes sickness and shortens life" and "beer is just as harmful as whiskey, and any consumption of either is injurious to the cells." As early as 1901, a state committee had declared that this information was "misleading, inaccurate, and unscientific," but the state's anti-alcohol forces were strong enough to overcome such sober reasoning. After Prohibition, however, Virginia became a monopoly state, meaning that at the same time the government required schools to teach that alcohol is evil and poisonous, it was also selling said evil poison to their parents. So in 1936, the Virginia legislature resolved to replace the unscientific anti-scientific propaganda with solid scientific study "as a basis for material to be taught in the public schools, accurate information as to the effect and use of alcohol upon the human system, in respect to both moderate and excessive use."

It commissioned a pair of scientists from the University of Virginia and the Medical College of Virginia to write a report on alcohol that could serve as the basis for a renewed curriculum for the state's schools. A year later, the scientists' work was done, and what they offered was hardly a pro-alcohol document. The scientists warned that

> alcohol depresses inhibitory control. This is the most acute effect of all those produced by alcohol. Hence, under its influence a person very early loses the usual restraints that have made him reserved, quiet and considerate of others. He may now betray secrets, exhibit vulgarity and become ill-mannered. It is well said that "there is truth

in wine" for being released from this controlling influence the individual betrays his real personality as it would be if he were to be stripped of the influences of inheritance and education. Dr. Jekyll becomes Mr. Hyde.

They described the person under the influence of alcohol as like a "decapitated crab" that "will use its claws to force food into its mouth and continue to swallow until its stomach actually bursts open."

Yet their report acknowledged, almost in passing, that in small amounts—such as a single shot of whiskey, bottle of beer, or glass of wine—it's harmless, and it's a bad idea to teach children otherwise. From the state's temperance-influenced educational materials on the subject, the scientists wrote, a student would receive

> only transient fear. He is taught that alcohol regardless of all consideration of time and frequency of ingestion, of quantity and concentration, and of age and state of health is a poison and as such always produces terrible effects; that the dire consequences of overindulgence are the sequels to any consumption whatsoever. At some time later in life the pupil observes that all those who use alcoholic beverages are not drunkards, and do not misbehave, are not sick, and do not 'go' crazy. The resulting influence on the young mind is far from wholesome.

The state board of education immediately accepted the scientists' report and approved its adoption in Virginia schools, calling it a "most valuable contribution . . . scientifically sound and very scholarly." *Virginia Medical Monthly* hailed it for telling "the truth about alcohol and its action on various systems of the body." The *Richmond Times-Dispatch* obtained a copy and ran a short article on its front page. In an editorial, the paper observed that the report

> leaves not the slightest doubt that the use of alcohol at any time and in other than in what may be termed microscopic volume is physically unwise and morally dangerous. Short of maintaining the untenable view that alcohol should never be used in any quantity for any purpose, the preponderant testimony given against strong drink

in the book makes it as strong a paper as any temperance organization could desire.

But the headline for the story was DEMON RUM DETHORNED IN TEXTBOOK and its lead bellowed, "The Demon Rum, heretofore presented to school children as a monster per se, will be introduced to Virginia schools as a beverage generally harmless in moderation, if a new textbook approved by the State Board of Education is adopted by the General Assembly for public use."

To the state's anti-alcohol activists, it read like an endorsement for booze, and their response was fast and furious. Churches passed around petitions, gathering thousands of signatures against what Virginia Anti-Saloon League superintendent Ed J. Richardson called the "very dangerous doctrine of moderation." State legislators were besieged with protest and, without having read the report, they stood to condemn it. Senator Vivian Page proclaimed: "Whisky is a drug that could not be handled in moderation," adding: "We should teach the children of Virginia that they should never touch a drop of alcohol as long as they live and that their first drink will be their worst."

Senator Leonard G. Muse, who during Prohibition had boasted from the Senate floor that he had drunk whiskey with "perhaps 95 percent" of his fellow legislators, said, "I understand that its general import is to discredit the use of alcohol, but certain scientific facts included in it, if not understood, may be damaging and misleading to young minds."

The senators voted unanimously to exclude the unread report from schools. When the measure moved to the House, a few representatives floated resolutions to at least be able to see the report before it was destroyed, but the outcry from the state's dry organizations intensified, and as the report was delivered to representatives, its ink barely dry, they voted unanimously to have all one thousand copies shoveled into the statehouse furnace and burned at a cost of nearly $1,000. (Though it was a public document and it had already been leaked, journalists' requests for copies were refused.) Still, the authors retained the copyright, and it was published by William Byrd Press in Richmond, where it ran through three printings. It was reviewed in early 1939 by the anti-alcohol *Scientific Temperance Journal*, which gave the book a not unfavorable assessment. The reviewer bristled at the work's assertion that moderate drinking carried no imminent danger but conceded that "sufficient evidence is given in the text for any normal minded pupil who does any thinking for himself to find ample proof that alcohol is better left alone."

The *Times-Dispatch* reported on the legislature's folly with appropriate bemusement. The national wire services picked up the story and spread it across the country. It caught the attention of some of the nation's top scientists, who rightly saw it as an attack on science, and it became a catalyst for the US scientific community to take an interest in the problem of the problem drinker.

Scientific Sleight of Hand

Around the same time Bill Wilson met with John D. Rockefeller Jr. in hopes of securing funds to address the problem of problem drinking in America, a group of prominent scientists met with the billionaire for much the same reason that Wilson had.

Spurred by the Virginia legislature's burning of a scientific report about alcohol and amid the nationwide groundswell of support for a return to Prohibition, nearly one hundred top scientists from universities across the country (including a pair of Nobel laureates) formed the Research Council on Problems of Alcohol. A subsidiary of the American Association for the Advancement of Science, the world's largest and most influential scientific society, the council would operate as a kind of brokerage house for research, evaluating and approving projects and dispensing funds, and, from their findings, sensible policies would emerge. "If we are to find a way out" of the alcohol problem, the AAAS's executive director declared at a New York press conference announcing the council's formation, "it can only be through the development of a complete factual basis on which can be built some effective plan of action."

The shift had begun with a decidedly dry campaign. At the time of repeal, all but one of the forty-eight states had on their books a requirement that schoolkids take classes on alcohol, but these courses, filled with scare tactics and blatantly false science, had been scaled back in most schools to a handful of perfunctory lectures or phased out completely. Here drys saw an opportunity to revamp the lessons with good science (which they felt certain would fall squarely against alcohol) and teach a new generation to loathe and fear liquor.

In Washington, DC, Harry Hascell Moore led the effort. During the 1920s, Moore had won acclaim in his service on President Herbert Hoover's Committee on the Costs of Medical Care, which gave rise to the United States' private insurance system, and in the early 1930s he published *We Are the Builders of a New World: A Summons to Youth*, an idealistic call for young Americans to embrace the challenges of the Great Depression as an opportunity. He founded in 1937 a group called the Sponsoring Committee of the National Conference on Alcohol and chose as members "scientists, business men and educators" who were either dry or dry leaning. Among them were several leaders of an organization called Allied Youth that formed youth groups across the country devoted to "having a good time without indulgence in alcohol." Another was Ray Lyman Wilbur, president of Stanford University and outspoken prohibitionist, who, at Moore's request, wrote a brief statement about the "alcohol problem" that revealed the committee's intentions:

> The steadily increasing use of beverage alcohol in this industrial age in America means an increase in accident, venereal disease, labor inefficiency, hospital and asylum costs. There is a direct relationship between all of these and the amount of alcohol which circulates in the blood of our people. Our boys and girls are entitled to a sane, reasonable, and unbiased presentation of all of the facts, favorable and unfavorable, regarding this narcotic, so that each may decide upon his own attitude toward its use.

But the Virginia book-burning incident had been an embarrassing setback, so Moore approached the AAAS in hopes that the venerable scientific society would lend credibility and attract funders. The AAAS leapt at the idea. Under the leadership of acclaimed astronomer F. R. Moulton, the AAAS had been looking for ways to expand science's social impact, to apply discovery to the benefit of humankind. Moore's project was made a subsidiary of the AAAS and renamed the Research Council on Problems of Alcohol, or RCPA, and its headquarters moved to New York.

Throughout the summer of 1938, more and more scientists signed on to the RCPA, and on October 2 the organization held a press conference in New York. The bully pulpit was tall and strong, and its announcement landed on the front page of the *New York Times*, a long piece with a jump to page nine, most of it taken verbatim from its press release. But on the editorial page, the paper scoffed at the scientists' "extraordinary innocence." The *Union Signal*, official organ of the National Woman's Christian Temperance Union, jeered:

"It is breathtaking! The saloonkeeper must have scientific aid to see in the streets about his saloon hungry, unkempt children whose fathers patronize his place of business . . . But the Council is to *inform* these persons, naively expecting that all these things they daily see will be remedied."

Undeterred, they set about trying to raise funds, going first to Rockefeller, expecting him to bankroll their entire mission—a half million to cover first-year expenses and millions more for years to come. But he was less impressed with this august group of top scientists than he had been with the alcoholic nonscientists Bill Wilson had represented in his appeal for funds. Rockefeller gave the RCPA nothing.

Almost all other foundations and philanthropists followed suit. Alcohol, the scientists were quickly learning, was simply too hot-button an issue. The nation's top givers wanted nothing to do with it. There were no government funds available, either. All the RCPA could manage to scare up in its first year was a $25,000 grant from the Carnegie Foundation to round up all previous research on alcohol and report on what was known at that point.

There was, however, one group that was interested in helping out: the liquor industry. At first the scientists declined, but by the time of the RCPA's first annual meeting, they were open to the idea. There they discussed how they might accept liquor money without compromising the integrity of their work. Their solution: shift the RCPA's focus from alcohol to "the disease of alcoholism."

In strictly scientific terms, there was as yet no such disease, and they knew it: much of that meeting's minutes record a long argument over just what alcoholism is or might be. They adopted a statement defining an "alcoholic" as "a person who cannot or will not control his drinking, and needs thorough and systematic treatment." They acknowledged that science had determined little about it, that there was no way of knowing whether it was hereditary or if it developed over the course of one's life but concluded that "an alcoholic should be regarded as a sick person, just as one who is suffering from tuberculosis, cancer, heart disease, or any other serious chronic disorder. He should be looked upon as a person needing medical care instead of as one who is guilty of a moral or criminal offense."

Immediately they tabled all proposed studies of alcohol itself—almost all of the proposals they'd previously approved. They held their third annual meeting at the Commodore Hotel in New York on October 16, 1940. More than two hundred people attended, including eight journalists. The *New York Times* published a story the next day under the headline ALCOHOLISM SEEN AS A MAJOR AILMENT: MEDICAL SCIENCE MUST STUDY FUNDAMENTAL CAUSES OF THE HABIT, PSYCHIATRIST SAYS. The story mentioned that H. F. Wilkie, vice president of Joseph E. Seagram Company and brother of the presidential candidate Wendell Wilkie, was in attendance. He "presented the viewpoint of the distilling industry. He said his company was desirous of cooperating with the program outlined by the council and would like 'to operate in the fulfillment of the various experimental objectives which have arisen.'"

This was a major development in America's history with alcohol, and it was critical to the burgeoning alcoholism treatment movement that would build the nation's alcoholism policies and treatment system. For one, it gave scientific clout to the Silkworth theory about alcoholism, itself central to the "cure" offered by AA. And, under the influence of the alcohol industry, it shifted focus from alcohol as a dangerous drug to the segment of the population that abuses it.

Alcohol and Public Opinion

Just a few years into its mission to help the United States "find a way out" of its long battle over alcohol, the scientists at the RCPA were languishing, despite the liquor money. The group peaked with its 1940 annual meeting but then grew poorer and weaker by the year. It wasn't funding any studies of alcoholism, much less alcohol, which it had originally formed to examine, and members were spending most of their time arguing about what purpose the group served. At its executive meeting in June 1941, attendees spent hours debating again about the definition of alcoholism.

While what little liquor money they'd scrounged up wasn't nearly enough to fund even the alcoholism studies they hoped to conduct, it also came with strings. Liquor industry representatives bristled at the term "alcoholic," and they called for a ban on its use by RCPA, arguing that people don't call diabetes sugarism.

Nonetheless, the scientists tried to get more money from the liquor industry. In 1943 the group hosted a conference at the Commodore Hotel in New York on "The Treatment and Prevention of Alcoholism in Contemporary and Post-War Worlds," where the group's president, Anton J. Carlson of the University of Chicago, said that the group's funding "could and should" come from "the distillers, the brewers, and the winemakers." He proposed that the liquor interests reduce their advertising budgets by 10 percent and devote that money to the "research, education and therapy sponsored by our council." He proposed state liquor agencies do so as well.

But, he conceded, even a major increase of funds from alcohol businesses likely wouldn't be enough, because they were up against something even bigger: public opinion.

"Unfortunately, even with millions in our annual budget, our council cannot promise our fellow citizens tomorrow complete freedom from wanting alcoholic liquors, nor complete freedom from the fear of the sequelae of occasional inebriety and chronic alcoholism," Carlson said.

> Both stem from elements in human nature and in our environment—
> elements which, even when completely understood, may possibly not
> be completely controlled, except via the long and difficult path of
> education and eugenics. It should be clear to our fellow citizens that
> we cannot be satisfied either with our present ignorance, nor our
> present biased propaganda about the blessings and the curse of alco-
> holic liquors. We must drive for more understanding. When such
> understanding is at hand, maybe we will begin to behave like humans,
> without legislative compulsion.

In hopes of bringing about a new understanding of alcoholism, the RCPA hired a public relations expert to craft a plan for them. The flak, Dwight Anderson, public relations director for the New York State Medical Society and chair of the National Association of Publicity Directors, reached back to Benjamin Rush's "Inquiry into the Effects of Ardent Spirits upon the Human Body and Mind," and Magus Huss's *Alcoholismus Chronicus* to show that the notion of alcoholism as a disease had been around for more than a century, since long before the word *alcoholism* even entered our vocabulary. In the late eighteenth century and as the temperance movement gained strength in the late nineteenth century, a smattering of inebriate asylums sprang up around the country. But these were overshadowed by the campaign against alcoholism itself, and drunks garnered little sympathy.

"The fact that the ideas we wish to advance have been repeatedly expressed in scientific literature during the past 150 years without penetrating the shell of public indifference is not grounds for discouragement," Anderson wrote in his report. "As long as these ideas were confined within the covers of scientific publications, and remained in the terms of scientific formulation, they could not capture the public mind."

To counter this, Anderson proposed a four-point platform for a nation-wide campaign:

1. "That the problem drinker is a sick man, exceptionally reactive to alcohol."
2. "That he can be helped."
3. "That he is worth helping."
4. "That the problem is therefore a responsibility of the healing professions, as well as of the established health authorities and public generally."

For the RCPA, the advice came too late; in a few years the group would disband. But these four points, with a bit of editing and in the hands of a true public relations master, one of the greatest of the twentieth century, would transform America's understanding of and response to problem drinking.

Promotion Rather Than Attraction

Like the scientists of RCPA, Wilson and his small cadre of recovering alcoholics had been rebuffed by Rockefeller, and they too turned to PR for their plan B. Their idea was to publish a book that told the story of their fellowship and the miracle of sobriety that they'd helped one another achieve. Wilson took to the task with a driving passion, writing day and night and sharing drafts at the weekly meeting in his home and sending copies to Smith in Akron and the new group in Cleveland. The forty or so members at the time fought continually over what should and should not be included in the book. The fights were so fierce that Wilson often retreated to his apartment in a fury of resentment and frustration, staying up all night, writing with a pencil on a legal pad. Wilson and his colleagues battled incessantly over how much God should be woven through its pages. The New York members wanted minimal or no mention of God. The Ohio members wanted God front and center. "So we fought, bled and died our way through one chapter after another," Wilson recalled, and their compromise was to evoke a God "of our understanding"—a "higher power," so as to allow agnostics and atheists to join and find sobriety with them.

During the months he was writing the book, Wilson took the train back and forth between New York and Akron, and on one of the journeys he took the Oxford Group's plan of action—which hinged on a five-step process of moral realignment known as the "Five Procedures": (1) Give in to God, (2) listen to God's directions, (3) to check guidance, (4) restitution, and (5) sharing, or telling one's sins—and turned them into a set of steps just for alcoholics. After a few drafts, he had a list of twelve, a number that seemed "a good significant figure in Christianity and mystic lore" and called to mind the twelve apostles.

The early members also debated how to characterize alcoholism. Midway through an early draft, Wilson asked cofounder Dr. Smith his opinion as to the accuracy of the disease label for alcoholism. Smith scribbled out a reply: "Have to use disease—sick—only way to get across hopelessness," underlining hopelessness for emphasis. This was hardly a true scientific validation. Smith was, after all, a proctologist, not a pathologist, and there was no evidence to support him even if he were. Rather, it was a kind of trick to scare alcoholics into abstinence and a spiritual course of remedy. It was part of the cure—the key to the first step AA members would have to take in their recovery—acceptance of powerlessness over alcohol.

To drive the notion of powerlessness home, they got Dr. Silkworth to contribute a chapter called "A Doctor's Opinion." In it, he described alcoholism as an allergy. "We believe," he wrote of himself and, ostensibly, his colleagues in the medical field, "that the action of alcohol on these chronic alcoholics is a manifestation of an allergy; that the phenomenon of craving is limited to this class and never occurs in the average temperate drinker. These allergic types can never safely use alcohol in any form at all; and once having formed the habit and found they cannot break it, once having lost their self-confidence, their reliance upon things human, their problems pile up on them and become astonishingly difficult to solve."

This concept of alcoholism as a physical ailment was so important to the program of recovery detailed in the book that they put Silkworth's chapter at the very beginning of the text. In order to stop drinking altogether and embrace a process based on faith in God, alcoholics had to not only understand but believe to the core of their being that they suffer from a physical ailment that makes it impossible for them to drink even the smallest amount of alcohol without falling inevitably into a full-blown binge.

After the preface by Silkworth, the book's first chapter tells Wilson's story from his first drink to his flash-of-light miracle to his early days of sobriety. It's followed by Smith's story, his creation of AA with Wilson, and then several chapters outlining the twelve-step course of action. The remainder of the book was filled with personal recovery stories by early members of AA, many of whom would fall away in relapse. Wilson gave the book a working title of *Alcoholics Anonymous*, and when members of a newly formed Cleveland group received drafts to review, they claimed the title as their name and Wilson kept it. In time, the title became the name of their growing organization and the book itself came to be known as the Big Book, because when it came time to have the tome printed, Wilson ordered the thickest paper available and it came back so fat the name fit and stuck.

Wilson and about fifty other early AA members had pooled together several thousand dollars to pay for *Alcoholics Anonymous* to be printed, and they were eager to be repaid on their investment and to begin amassing funds for their mission to help still-suffering alcoholics across the nation and world. They sent copies to doctors nationwide, and the response was tepid at best and at worst insultingly dismissive. The *Journal of the American Medical Association* wrote that the book is "a curious combination of organizing propaganda and religious exhortation. It is in no sense a scientific book" and of "no scientific merit or interest." The *Journal of Nervous and Mental Disease* jeered at its "regressive mass psychological method" and "religious fervor" and described it as "a rambling sort of camp-meeting" with a lack of solid information about alcoholism: "It's all surface material."

There were some good reviews. The *New England Journal of Medicine* wrote that "the authors have presented their case well, in fact, in such good style that it may be of considerable influence when read by alcoholic patients." And a writer for the *New York Times* deemed it "more soundly based psychologically than any other treatment of the subject." (Though the writer conceded in conclusion that "it is a strange book.") But the reviews, good or bad, were few and far between. Their work had inspired no news or feature stories, so sales stalled.

But they seemed to catch a big break when one of their newest members, an Irishman by the name of Morgan Ryan, reached out to someone who knew someone who hosted a national radio program, and he managed to schedule an on-air interview. At first Wilson and the other members were thrilled at the prospect. "Then all of a sudden, we had a big chill," Wilson would later recall in a speech at an AA convention. "We thought, well suppose this Irishman got drunk before" the interview? "So we rented a room in the downtown Athletic Club and we put Ryan in there with a day-and-night guard for ten days."

Meantime, with Ryan safely sequestered, Wilson and the other early members sought to capitalize on the opportunity by spending $500—the sum total of the group's treasury—to buy and mail postcards to doctors across the country, alerting them to the upcoming radio show and advertising their book, *Alcoholics Anonymous*, as "a sure-cure for alcoholism."

Under lock and key, their radio evangelist Ryan managed to stay sober (though he later relapsed and dropped out of AA). Wilson and his fellow AA members were giddy at the prospect of thousands of orders for their new book. To allow the postcards to pile up, they waited three days before venturing to the post office to collect their bounty. Then, as Wilson would recall, "We go to the clerk, and he brings out twelve lousy postal cards, ten of them completely illegible, written by doctors, druggists, monkeys, and we had exactly two orders of the book and we were absolutely and utterly stone broke."

Wilson worked to drum up more publicity and seemed to catch a break when an editor at *Reader's Digest* promised a glowing feature about the book and the organization. But months passed with no article. The less-popular *Liberty* magazine ran an article called "Alcoholics and God" and *Time* published a short review of the Big Book, and these articles brought in hundreds of letters to AA's New York headquarters from alcoholics looking for help, among them a few orders for books. But it wasn't enough to pay back their investments for the book, let alone fund their ambitious, world-saving plans.

They went back to John D. Rockefeller Jr., and he offered to host a dinner for them, to which he would invite wealthy donors like himself. Rockefeller couldn't attend and instead sent his son Nelson Rockefeller, who doused their dreams by telling the potential donors that AA is "a great and wonderful thing," but that it "proceeds on goodwill. It requires no money."

Meantime, the new Cleveland AA group members persuaded the *Plain Dealer* to come check them out, and this resulted in a six-part series that boosted membership in their area. Among the new arrivals was Rollie Hemsley, a catcher for the Cleveland Indians whose drunken antics had earned him the nicknames "the Rollicker" and "Rollicking Rollie." He often insulted fans and sprayed seltzer on them, he'd thrown a punch at a cop, and he'd smashed a journalist on the head with a dresser drawer. But famed Cleveland fastball hurler Bob Feller swore Hemsley played better drunk than most catchers played sober. On a 1939 road trip, Hemsley got plastered and doused a sleeping porter with water and went up and down the sleeping cars tossing lit matches into his teammates' beds before climbing into the sack with the Indians' manager, Ossie Vitt, who suspended him. During his suspension, Hemsley read the *Plain Dealer*'s series on AA and reached out for help. On opening day of the 1940 season he caught a no-hitter by Feller and hit a triple that brought in the game's only run. At the press conference afterward, he said, "I've quit drinking" and credited AA: "I haven't had a drink in a year and I want others to know the reason why, so they can be helped."

The wires picked up Hemsley's story, and more inquiries came into AA from across the nation. Still, Wilson wanted more, a monumental national breakout. Above all, he longed for an article in the *Saturday Evening Post*, the most popular magazine in the country. Again and again he pitched his story to the editor, who was intrigued but skeptical; the editor gave the assignment to one of his toughest investigative reporters, Jack Alexander, who took on the assignment expecting it to be an exposé of a cult. But Wilson and his fellow members welcomed Alexander in, took him to meetings in New York and Akron and Cleveland, and Alexander started to think maybe AA was all right after all. He got in touch with a couple of reporters who had gotten sober through the program, and they assured him it was the real deal. When Alexander's article hit the stands in March 1941, AA's membership was at about two thousand. By the end of that year, it had swelled to eight thousand, with new groups popping up from California to Maine.

But these numbers were nothing compared to the growth that would come when their program of promotion rather than attraction fell into the hands of one of the great PR geniuses of the twentieth century, who would take up the campaign.

The First Lady of Alcoholics Anonymous

If you walk into any AA club in the world, you're likely to see framed pictures of Bill Wilson and Robert Smith hanging on the wall. As AA's founders, they're credited with bringing the Twelve Steps into the world and leading millions to sobriety. Both men are the subjects of several biographies, and they were immortalized in a made-for-TV movie. But credit for AA's explosive worldwide growth belongs not to them but to a woman few members of AA know anything about: Marty Mann.

She'd grown up privileged. Her father was a top executive for the Marshall Field & Co. department store. She attended the prestigious college preparatory academy Chicago Latin School. Ambitious, she wanted to be a writer, and as a child she set out to write the great American novel. But when she was about to enter high school, she came down with tuberculosis. At the time, in the early 1920s, TB was looked on as a lower-class disease, an affliction of the poor. Her parents shipped her off to the Barlow Sanatorium in Los Angeles. They didn't tell her what she had, fearing she wouldn't be able to keep it secret and in telling others would embarrass the family.

The commitment did little to improve her condition, largely because, in her ignorance of her illness, she wouldn't cooperate with treatment. Exasperated, her doctor told her what she had and that she would die if she didn't follow the regimen of rest, diet, and fresh air and sunlight. She was shocked and dismayed at being so deceived; she hadn't chosen to become ill, she was a passive victim of the disease. She recovered, but the injustice of the experience remained with her for her entire life, helping shape her ultimate life's mission: to remove the stigma from alcoholism, which she would come to understand as a disease that can afflict anyone, just like tuberculosis.

Her family liked to drink. Her parents, Will and Lilly, enjoyed cocktails every evening, and she had her first taste of alcohol at a young age—at holiday events such as Christmas and Thanksgiving. At the onset of Prohibition, her father stocked their cellar with several years' worth of wine and whiskey. In her early twenties, Mann began making a habit of drinking. On a trip to New Orleans for Mardi Gras, she met a man at a party who liked drinking as much as she did, and on impulse she married him. But their marriage fell apart as quickly as it had come together, in part because they both drank too much but also because Mann identified as a lesbian.

After the split, she kept her ex's last name, and she kept drinking too. By all accounts, she was a pro. A "well-known writer who squired her to speakeasies and fabulous parties" would later tell Reader's Digest: "I can't ever remember dating a more beautiful and intelligent girl. And how she could drink! A hollow leg, that girl!"

When her father lost his money in the Depression and was no longer able to support her, she moved to New York to find work, settling in Greenwich Village. There she shared a flat with two other young women, began writing art book reviews, and then became a magazine editor at *International Studio*. Through the Roaring Twenties she thrived in the media and publishing world, where alcohol was a kind of lifeblood. Her grandmother passed away, leaving her some money, and in 1930, she moved to England and fell in with the so-called Bloomsbury Set, getting to know Virginia Woolf, Nancy Cunard, and others. On trips to Paris she'd visit Gertrude Stein's salon.

On the Fourth of July 1934, at a big party in the country, she began drinking on an empty stomach, and by midafternoon she was staggering drunk. Some friends led her upstairs to sleep it off. Her room had French doors leading to a balcony, and she stumbled off of it, smacking hard against the flagstone patio below. Barely thirty, she nearly died from the fall (or jump, she would never be able to remember which), fracturing her leg at the hip, breaking her jaw at both hinges. For the next six months she lay in traction but still kept drinking. She'd beg friends to smuggle whiskey into the hospital. With her mouth wired shut, she had to drink it through a straw.

Upon release, she stayed in London and fell back into daily drinking, bouncing from job to job until no one would hire her, and she spent her days holed up in a Hyde Park flat, too sloshed most of the time to get up from bed. Twice she tried to kill herself. Friends urged her to stop drinking, and one even fell on his knees and begged, but she wouldn't—or couldn't.

She left England, fleeing back to the States, to New York, in hopes that the change in scenery would sober her up, but it didn't work and she wound up, in her own words, "utterly alone and broke, there was nothing left to do but drink . . . and drink . . . and drink."

A friend got her an appointment with a top psychologist, head of the neurology department at Bellevue, who in turn got her a bed at a private sanitarium in Connecticut, under the care of a psychologist named Dr. Harry Tiebout, who took her on pro bono as part of his research on alcoholism. She stayed for a year, doing everything Tiebout told her to do, taking every pill he prescribed, sitting through hour after hour of therapy sessions, but invariably she would sneak away to get drunk.

Nothing seemed to work, and both doctor and patient were about to give up when Tiebout gave her a manuscript with a red cardboard cover bound with cord, a book written by and for alcoholics—the as-yet unpublished *Alcoholics Anonymous*. Maybe this would help, Tiebout suggested.

At first as she read it, she felt great relief. The stories the authors told of their hopeless battles with alcoholism seemed exactly like her own. And the book described her condition as an allergy. This struck her like a thunderbolt. Her heavy drinking wasn't her fault. She wasn't weak-willed and morally flawed. She was sick, like she had been when she came down with TB. The revelation was liberating.

Yet the cure spelled out in the manuscript's pages seemed unpalatable to her. As she flipped through, the word God appeared over and over, and she recoiled. She was atheist, proudly so, a modern woman. What's more, the book was all about men. She grew angrier and angrier as she read, and finally she threw the manuscript across the room.

The book landed on her bed and fell open. As she would later recall many times, "in the middle of the page was a line that stood out as if carved in raised block letters, black, high, sharp—'We cannot live with anger.'"

She seemed to lose consciousness for a moment, and when she came to she found herself kneeling at her bedside, praying. She felt her body become light, filled with serenity and well-being.

She went to Dr. Tiebout. "Have I lost my mind?" she asked him. "Am I insane?"

"Perhaps you had a genuine spiritual experience," he replied.

That did it. "Somehow those words were the battering ram that knocked down my resistance," she'd later say. She sat down and read the book again. By the end she felt the first hope she'd felt in many years.

After checking out of the sanitarium, Mann returned to New York and connected with Bill Wilson, author of the book that had given her hope. He took her to AA meetings and became a kind of mentor for her recovery—a sponsor, in AA parlance. The people she met at the meetings were skeptical, not only because she was the only woman among them but also because she was so young. Their understanding of the disease of alcoholism was that a person had to suffer for years before he or she was ready for the cure.

"When I attended my first AA meeting in April, 1939, I noticed that there was a sort of sad look on a number of faces," she would later recall.

They shook their heads just a little bit. They all asked me how old I was. I was in my very early thirties. None of them looked convinced I was ever going to be seen again, and I asked why they looked skeptical; and they told me that I was too young. They had had no success with anyone under forty. They didn't believe they could help anyone who had not hit bottom. . . . They didn't believe that a woman in her early thirties could have hit bottom. They didn't know I had!

She relapsed several times during her first year, once for a ten-day binge, but she kept coming back to meetings. She worked for a spell as fashion publicity director at Macy's department store, where she met Priscilla Peck, copywriter for the company. Peck was a recovering alcoholic as well, and they quickly fell in love and moved into a stylish Manhattan apartment together. As Mann strung together days and weeks and months of continuous sobriety, she became a kind of unpaid salesperson for AA. Her public relations skills were well suited to the task, and she began giving speeches to civic clubs and religious groups. Jack Alexander interviewed her for his *Saturday Evening Post* article. He gave her the pseudonym Sarah Martin, and after the article came out, she felt exhilarated by the way her story had served to help others with alcohol problems learn of a way out. One day as she was walking along Fifth Avenue, she looked up at all the windows in the apartments and wondered how many people living in them were struggling with alcohol. "I wanted to reach each one," she would later recall. "I wanted to help each one—but how?"

One sleepless night, she prayed for guidance, asking God: "Give me something useful to do." Inspiration came to her at once, and she leaped out of bed, raced to her typewriter and started typing. Out came her life's mission: to change the way the world conceives of problem drinking and to lead every suffering alcoholic to AA.

2 | 1944–1953: THE DISEASE GOES VIRAL

Wheelhorse of the Movement

In Marty Mann, the earliest members of AA would find exactly what they would later claim to have never needed: a tireless, media-savvy promoter of their fledgling movement. She met Wilson for coffee and shared with him her vision for a national public relations campaign to educate America about the disease of alcoholism and its cure—AA. He loved the idea, but he doubted she could pull it off. What she'd need, he said, was scientific backing; people wouldn't buy the idea of problem drinking as illness unless there were scientific proof of some kind. To get it, Mann first went to the Research Council on Problems of Alcohol. She and Wilson had attended the council's third annual meeting in 1940, and an earlier PR job had brought her into contact with Jack Anderson, who had advised the group on ways to promote the unproven notion that alcoholism is a disease. She laid out her plan. The scientists at RCPA were interested, but the sparse funds they'd received from the liquor industry weren't enough to pay for the kind of PR campaign Mann had in mind.

They told her that there was, however, an organization that did have sufficient resources: Yale University. There, a professor of physiology named Howard Haggard had recently founded a school for the study of alcohol. Haggard was one of the best-known scientists of his day—author of bestselling popular science books such as *Staying Young Beyond Your Years*, *The Doctor in History*, and *Devils, Drugs and Doctors*. He hosted a weekly radio show on CBS and was a favorite source for reporters. He wasn't afraid to turn conventional wisdom on its head (example from the *Times*, June 9, 1938: CROSS CHILDREN SHOULD GET CANDY, NOT SCOLDINGS, DOCTOR DECLARES; IT RESTORES DEPLETED ENERGIES, DR. HAGGARD EXPLAINS). He'd conducted some research on alcohol, studying its metabolization in the body, and he'd very publicly opposed Prohibition, arguing that Americans need to understand and accept that alcohol, used in moderation, is not only safe, but it's normal. He was an advocate of moderate drinking and referred to it often in his writings and public speeches. He'd joined the RCPA after the Virginia legislature report burning. But when the RCPA capitulated to liquor interests, agreeing to study not alcohol but the undefined disease of alcoholism, he quit and established his own program at Yale.

When Haggard left, he took with him a young scientist named Elvin Morton "Bunky" Jellinek, who had been hired by the RCPA to conduct the study of all previous alcohol studies, which had been funded with a $25,000 grant from the Carnegie Foundation. Before signing on with the RCPA, Jellinek had worked as a biometrician in Sierra Leone, where he studied plants, then in Honduras, where he studied fruit for the United Fruit Company, and finally at a hospital in Hartford, Connecticut, where he was researching schizophrenia when he came into contact with the RCPA. He'd also at one point studied the ethnographic history of the shoe. His CV boasted an honorary doctorate from Leipzig University, but historians would later conclude that he fabricated this degree and quite possibly never received even a bachelor's degree. Despite this sketchy pedigree, Jellinek would come to be known as "the father of the disease concept of alcoholism."

Mann gathered up her plan to educate the public about "the disease of alcoholism," sealed it in an envelope, and sent it off to Jellinek in Connecticut.

Jellinek immediately seized on the idea. Having seen firsthand how difficult it had been, even with the AAAS's backing, for the RCPA to drum up support for a scientific approach to what was then referred to as "the alcohol problem," and eager for the Yale Plan on Alcohol to take off, he saw in Mann's query an opportunity to shift public attitudes about drinking and drinking problems. He took a train straightaway to New York to discuss it, and at his meeting with Mann he proposed more than just sponsorship. He wanted to incorporate Mann's campaign into the Yale program and to offer financial support so it could begin immediately.

"This will be the wheelhorse of our movement," he told his boss Haggard upon his return to New Haven. Haggard agreed and hired Mann right away.

It was an impulsive move, out of character because neither Haggard nor Jellinek fully believed the theory that alcoholism is a disease. In a book they'd cowritten, *Alcohol Explored*, published a couple years earlier by Doubleday, they stated in the opening chapter that they would avoid the word alcoholism because of the lack of scientific evidence of its existence. "The illness conception of alcoholism was not a central idea of the activities of the Yale group except in its summer school," sociologist Bruce Holley Johnson would later write about this move to embrace Mann's campaign. "And even there it was developed against a background of the widest span." Or as Ron Roizen, another sociologist, would later explain in a comprehensive study of the alcoholism movement: "In effect, then, Mann was asked to market a product [that its] putative producers viewed with ambivalence."

With the Yale alcohol program, Haggard and Jellinek had aimed to study alcohol problems in all their complexity. They'd brought on board Yale sociologist Selden Bacon, who helped them establish in 1943 the Yale Summer School of Alcohol Studies, a monthlong course of study into the drug's many facets and impacts on individuals and society as a whole. Hundreds of applications poured in for their first session—scientists, policy makers, community officials, doctors, liquor industry representatives, and leaders from the temperance movement. Seventy attended this five-week session, sitting in on lectures and panel discussions on "The Problems of Alcohol," "Alcohol and Complex Society," and "Medical Treatment of the Inebriate." The curriculum included "physiology; national and class liquor attitudes and practices; traffic problems; relations of personality to alcohol; suicide, crime; heredity; temperance movements; social control; legislation; church strategy." The school included twenty lecturers, and students included "clergymen, probation officers, school administrators, teachers, welfare workers."

The first conference drew a fair amount of media attention, and the reporters who covered it had fun with the novelty of wets and drys convening. "No one swung an ax at gleaming glassware in the manner of" nineteenth-century dry crusader Carrie Nation, *Newsweek* reported.

No one sang darkly of 'King Al Kee Hall' in the manner of the '20s and early '30s. Now the Drys were convinced that a scientific approach would prove a more practical weapon against Demon Rum than physical violence. The Wets believed that their side, too, would get valuable ammunition from even a brief education in all phases of the effects and non effects of alcohol. And members of churches and social agencies who sat on the fence between the two extremes agreed it was high time the alcohol problem were attacked with the brain instead of the bludgeon.

The magazine *Collier's* also sent a reporter and photographer up to New Haven to check the school out. In the top photo of the three-page spread, Jellinek was shown standing between Virginia Colvin, daughter of D. Leigh Colvin, the 1936 Prohibition candidate for president, and Merle Hagemeyer of Seagram Distillers, both of them much taller than him. "Our object is not to convert anyone to any point of view," he was quoted as saying. "We wish only to explore the problems of alcohol." He added: "We present facts, and the student can make use of them as he sees fit."

Reaction was mixed. "It's the biggest step forward in a century," Nathan Adler of the Mental Hygiene Society of Northern California said of the school. "Within a few years, this School can change the whole temperance attitude of the country." On the other hand, O. G. Christgau of the Anti-Saloon League in Iowa declared: "All that I've heard made me doubly sure that Prohibition must return."

"I am not interested in a man who has ever drunk so much whiskey that he had a hangover the next morning," the Rev. W. D. Bayley told the reporters. "The sooner that man and others like him die from a cobbled liver, the better off society will be."

But the overall theme was collegiality and cooperation, a shared sense that objectivity and clearheadedness would lead America out of the long fight over alcohol. The overall lesson seemed to be that alcohol abuse was less a problem of morality and more an issue of pathology. "Many students were surprised to learn that there is virtual unanimity among psychiatrists in believing that 'problem drinking' is as much of a disease as cancer," *Newsweek* wrote. "Even so, it was revealed by Dr. Jellinek, 'it won't dawn on society as a whole for another 30 years.'"

Walter H. McKenzie, executive secretary of the United Texas Drys, concluded a report on his attendance with an open-minded and compassionate note:

> It has made me more understanding and sympathetic toward the alcoholic. I have not particularly changed my thinking concerning some of the dangers attending the Alcoholics Anonymous Movement, but I definitely understand it better and have a great deal more sympathy with the 750,000 alcoholics in the nation. I feel so keenly for them that I am willing to do anything I can to assist them in their program of rehabilitation.

The peace was short lived. After a couple summer sessions, the drys turned on Yale, branded it as a front for liquor interests, which Yale denied (despite receiving significant funds from a former student of Haggard's who had taken over his family's brewery in Minnesota). They published a pamphlet called the "Education Program of the Liquor Interests" that accused the Yale Summer School of being a scheme "to get as many Drys as possible out of circulation for four weeks" and that Yale "claims to be neither Wet nor Dry—which makes it WET."

An Auspicious Beginning

At its inception, the Yale Plan on Alcohol had four divisions:

1. Research into the physiological, sociological, medical, psychological, historic, legal, and clinical aspects of alcohol and problem drinking.
2. The *Quarterly Journal of Studies on Alcohol*, in which scientists could publish their research.
3. The Yale Summer School.
4. A clinic established in New Haven for the diagnosis and treatment of alcoholics and for research and training. It was intended as a pilot for clinics that would open across the country.

When Mann came on board, her campaign became their fifth division. Haggard offered her a grant to cover expenses for two years. In 1944, she attended the Yale Summer School of Alcohol Studies, spending her weekdays in New Haven and weekends in New York. Tensions arose from the start. She butted heads with a psychologist and doctoral student named Edith Gomberg, who felt that Mann was condescending to nonalcoholics. She seemed to believe that experience with the problem was paramount, that it trumped scientific know-how. And though Mann befriended D. Leigh Colvin of the National Woman's Christian Temperance Union, whom she was able to convince to accept the notion of alcoholism as a disease, other temperance advocates who attended the school were cold to the notion that alcoholics could and should be rehabilitated. "If I had my way," one told her, "I'd put them all on a boat and sink it."

With Yale's explicit stamp of scientific approval, Mann founded the National Committee for Education on Alcoholism (NCEA), setting up offices in Manhattan's Academy of Medicine. The location was chosen for its name, to drive home the point that alcoholism is a disease, not a moral failing. And on October 2, 1944, she formally announced her endeavor.

At the glitzy Biltmore Hotel in Manhattan, in a smart skirt suit and laced hat and flanked by scientists from Yale, she stood before reporters and photographers with cameras flashing from all the New York papers and the major national news services. She confessed to all the world that she was an alcoholic and that she had now "been free for five years. I was chosen for this office because as a recovered alcoholic I can supplement the scientists' knowledge of the problem. A main objective of our education program is to convince the public that alcoholism is a disease and the alcoholic is a sick person."

NCEA's platform was virtually the same four-point platform the RCPA had adopted several years earlier, on the advice of a PR consultant—that problem drinkers are sick men, that they can be helped, that they're worth helping, and that the public and medical community have a responsibility to help them. Mann, with her considerable knowledge of how to frame an idea for mass appeal, merely tightened the RCPA's platform, cutting it from four points to three, and removed all hedge words around the notion of alcoholism as an illness:

1. Alcoholism is a disease and the alcoholic is a sick person.
2. The alcoholic can be helped and is worth helping.
3. This is a public health problem and therefore a public responsibility.

All of New York's newspapers carried the story the next day, and the AP, UP, and INS news services brought the story to the rest of the country. The coverage continued for weeks. The press loved Mann; she gave good quotes, and she was gifted at the give and take (when a reporter called her an "ex-lady lush," she corrected him with tongue in cheek: "I might be an ex-lush, but I am definitely a lady!"). She offered something of a man-bites-dog story: drunkards aren't degenerates, they're sick. And they're not all wallowing on skid row. Many are well bred, well heeled, intelligent, articulate, like her, because she defied the common conception of alcoholics. In a glowing profile titled THE SICK PERSON WE CALL AN ALCOHOLIC, the *New York Times Magazine* described her as "an attractive, smart woman in her thirties. Her clear complexion, alert blue eyes and her manner bear no trace of years of hard drinking. . . . It was hard to believe she was talking about herself." *Time* also ran a feature about her and her group.

She also made it clear that this wasn't a new campaign in the old war between wet and dry. "Please don't get the idea that our committee is a crusading outfit going around the country with hatchets trying to smash up gin mills," she told reporters. "Those of us who are alcoholics are personal drys because we realize we can't take alcohol in moderation. But this does not mean we believe that those who can should be deprived of it. For us it is drunkenness or dryness. For those not afflicted as we are, to drink or not to drink is not such an important question."

More major articles appeared in *Time, Health, Look, True Story, Mademoiselle*—some of them written by members of AA themselves, though they didn't disclose their affiliation. The *New York World-Telegram* published, in the words of sociologist Bruce Holley Johnson, "a very well-written feature article on the NCEA in November 1944. The article, written by Douglas Gilbert, provided an in-depth presentation of the NCEA's key ideas and organizational objectives. It was, in total, a masterful piece of persuasive writing. What was missing from the public account of this story was the fact that Douglas Gilbert was himself a recovered alcoholic." Gilbert was, according to Johnson, "one of many members of the New York press corps who had serious drinking problems and had been helped by AA."

Media Sensation

On November 25, 1946, two years into her ever-expanding campaign, Marty Mann stepped to the podium at the Economic Club of Detroit, a distinguished platform for business and civic leaders of international renown. She was one of the first women ever to do so. "I stand before you here today on behalf of two groups," she began. "One group is made of free people, free because they have knowledge. The other group is made of prisoners, prisoners of their condition, held prisoners by ignorance and fear."

Dressed in a dark skirt suit and a feathery white hat, she paused to draw out the metaphor. "These prisoners," she said, "are the alcoholics of America, three million strong. Many of them are unaware of their condition; are unaware of its nature; and are unaware that there is anything whatsoever to do about it."

Again she paused, to play up the drama.

"I belonged to that group," she said matter-of-factly. "I myself shared their condition of being a prisoner until the truth set me free."

The Economic Club of Detroit was one of the biggest platforms she'd spoken from, a venue where world leaders broke news with bold policy pronouncements. Less than a minute into her address, which was simulcast on radio, she had the audience thoroughly entranced. It was startling to see this handsome, refined woman standing before them declaring, almost with pride, that she was an alcoholic. That was a term for the dregs of society, men who slept in gutters and begged for spare change.

She went on to say that she never chose to be an alcoholic. The condition had been foisted on her by fate. She was born that way, the victim of a disease. "The fact that alcoholism is a disease," she said, "has been known in science for over 150 years," and she identified herself as a representative of Yale, thus adding credibility and certitude to her scientific claim. Indeed she had been preceded on the stage by Bunky Jellinek, a bona fide scientist and one of the principals of Yale's Center of Alcoholism Studies. Almost in passing he referred to the "rise of the disease known as alcoholism" in his speech, which was titled "What Shall We Do About Alcoholism?: Cost to Business and Government," and was filled with figures about alcoholism's economic impact. But now Mann, in full command of the crowd, was leaning hard into this notion, which Jellinek and his Yale colleagues knew full well was without proof.

Mann's speech, titled "Alcoholics Anonymous," focused mainly on the hope that the organization offered to those afflicted with alcoholism. "Alcoholics don't get help because they're stigmatized," she said.

> Not until the creation of Alcoholics Anonymous twelve years ago was there any change in this situation. No one any longer can say as I myself once said and as we all were taught, that the drunkard is a bum for whom there is no hope because there is something vital missing in him—or he would not let himself get that way.
>
> I think you can understand that when this thing began to happen to me it was simply not possible for me to identify myself with that picture. How could someone with my background, with my upbringing, with my education, how could someone like that have this happen?

Mann gave a variation of this speech hundreds of times in dozens of cities. She appeared before the South Carolina House of Representatives. In her first year on the job, Mann flew back and forth across the country, logging more than thirty thousand miles to give speeches to civic groups in communities large and small. (Of her grueling schedule she quipped, "Somehow I survived my own program—mostly on Hershey bars and milk snatched while doing a vaudevillian quick-change. I deeply regret being a woman on such occasions: clothes, hair-dos and makeup unnecessarily complicate one's life.") She gave more than four hundred talks to an estimated one hundred thousand people and appeared on thirty-eight radio talk shows, three of which broadcast to national audiences, carrying her message to an estimated twenty-five million listeners. In his dissertation about the modern alcoholism movement, Johnson tallied the annual number of major magazine articles about alcoholism as a disease during this time period. From 1935 to 1944, the number that would appear each year was in the single digits. In 1945, the first full year of Mann's campaign, there were fifteen. The next year there were twenty-two, and they stayed in the double digits into the mid-1960s.

Hollywood took notice, too. In 1944, Billy Wilder directed *The Lost Weekend*, based on a book written by Charles Jackson, an alcoholic who was in and out of AA for much of his life. In it, the main character, Don, is described as "a sick person. It's as though something were wrong with his heart or liver."

After its runaway success, Mann landed a job working as a consultant for another film about alcoholism, *Smash-Up: The Story of a Woman*, written by Dorothy Parker (who was an early board member of NCEA) and released in 1947. Mann read the script and corresponded with the producer during pre-production and then flew to L.A. to coach the lead actress, Susan Hayward.

Smash-Up was more explicit in its depiction of alcoholism as a disease than *The Lost Weekend*. At its climax, a doctor tells the husband of Hayward's character, "Your wife is the victim of a disease and there is only one cure. That is to give up liquor entirely. They're like diabetics who must give up sugar and take insulin. Alcoholics must give up alcohol." Before she's ready to do so, however, she passes out with a lit cigarette and burns down her house, nearly killing her child and disfiguring her own face with burns. In the end, finally sober, she tells her husband, "I needed to hit rock bottom before I could change. Now I . . . I'm never going to be afraid again."

Mann's fast and furious work around the country very quickly had an effect. In 1949, a professor at Rutgers conducted surveys on public opinion about alcoholism and found that 36 percent of respondents believed that alcoholism is a disease, whereas when he'd conducted the same survey four years earlier, a mere 5 percent believed this.

The Yale Clinics

While Mann was crisscrossing the country, spreading her story about the disease of alcoholism and its cure, Haggard and his colleagues at Yale were trying to write their own. With help from the state of Connecticut, they opened two clinics for alcoholics in New Haven and Hartford. Their staffs consisted of one full-time psychiatrist, two internists to assist with medical concerns and give physical examinations, two psychiatric social workers, a receptionist, and a clerk. Outside specialists were also brought in to assist with laboratory and psychological tests when necessary. Initially, the clinics handled about twenty-five cases per month. One-third came from court referrals, another third from social agencies, and a third from self-referrals, AA, and public welfare agencies.

The goal was "to test on a small scale the possibilities of large-scale rehabilitation of inebriates at a cost which would be not only within the means of a community but far below the costs involved in arrests, jailing, mental-hospital care, public support of dependents, and losses due to accidents and absenteeism," Jellinek wrote in a report on the first six months of the clinics' operation. The project was justified, he explained, "by the medical view that inebriety is an ailment."

When patients came in, they were given a physical, asked to give as thorough a "drinking history" as possible, and told to return for several visits over the course of two weeks. From this data, the clinic's staff developed an individualized plan. The program of treatment followed the "general principles of psychotherapy," according to the clinics' training materials, and the primary goal was to help the patients understand that alcohol wasn't their problem but rather the results of underlying problems that led them to drink compulsively, such as mental illness and stress. The clinics' staff would work with them to develop new ways of coping with these underlying problems so as to enable them to break free from their excessive drinking.

"All patients are informed of the activities of Alcoholics Anonymous and, if they seem suitable, are encouraged to join the organization," the clinics' documents say, but AA was just one remedy the clinic employed. The clinics' director, Raymond McCarthy, didn't believe there was a "generalized treatment approach" or "single therapy" for alcoholism. He believed "there is no alcoholic as such," but rather "thousands of individuals who persist in using alcohol after they have demonstrated that they cannot control its use."

"Very few alcoholics can actually be typified," wrote Carney Landis, one of the lecturers at the Yale school. "In fact, all of the studies which have been made thus far lead to the conclusion that there is no unitary grouping of personality traits or attitudes which truly characterizes any considerable number of individuals addicted to the use of alcohol."

These scientists believed that there was likely a physiological aspect to alcoholism, but they knew there was as yet no evidence to back up the claim— contrary to what Mann was saying in her appearances around the country. "There are many forms of treatment for alcoholism and, for all, recoveries are claimed and, no doubt, obtained," Haggard wrote in an article describing their efforts. "It cannot be shown that there is a common etiology for excessive drinking." So "the Yale Plan Clinics emphasized experimental treatment approaches," according to Sally Brown, Marty Mann's biographer. "The bulk of these approaches were psychological, but also included investigations into physiology and nutrition. Yale considered four avenues of psychological treatment—lay therapy, psychiatry, condition reflex (aversion therapy), and AA."

The clinics encouraged their patients to pursue abstinence, but short of that they would urge them to reduce their consumption. "If an inebriate can be helped to reduce his habitual two or more bouts of intoxication per week to an occasional occurrence of once or twice in three months, his health as well as his economic condition will be greatly improved," they wrote in their training materials. "Furthermore, in learning to face his problems for several weeks or months at a time without inebriation the patient learns that 'it can be done,' and there is a chance to create permanent sobriety. Finally, if the clinic takes the patient back after an occasional slip, he does not seem to have more reason for losing courage than the clinic has."

All of these approaches explored by the Yale clinics—especially the openness to reducing the patients' drinking—were very different from the message Marty Mann was spreading on Yale's behalf. Indeed, correspondence in Mann's archives reveals that she didn't think too highly of her benefactors' medical endeavors. Of Yale's efforts, Mann wrote to a fellow member of AA, "Not that I, as a dyed-in-the-wool AA, believe that clinics, or any other medical or psychiatric means can straighten out very many 'alkies,'" adding: "but I do believe the average person will more readily go into a clinic to find out what to do for what ails them than they will investigate a layman's organization such as ours. And I also believe that the very presence of a clinic will emphasize and advertise to the uninitiated that alcoholism is a disease which is to be treated, not hidden or punished."

AA by Any Other Name

Yale University was ostensibly Mann's main client; it funded her efforts and loaned its institutional clout. But in truth the NCEA wasn't working for Yale, promoting its study of alcohol through Haggard's program. It was working on behalf of AA, and in the beginning Mann made no secret about it. She decided early on, after much thought and deliberation, to identify herself at all of her public appearances as an alcoholic and to credit AA with her recovery. It wasn't an easy decision. She feared that the move might endanger her own sobriety by feeding her ego and setting her up for a fall. And if that happened, she feared a relapse by a well-known AA member such as herself would cause the public to doubt the organization's efficacy. She conferred with Wilson and her new colleagues at Yale, and they all agreed that she should risk the consequences because her personal story was such a powerful tool of persuasion.

She didn't relapse, at least not at that point in her venture, but her break with AA's tradition of secrecy did spark an uproar among AA's membership. In addition to the potential for an image-damaging relapse, AA members became suspicious that her organization was a self-aggrandizing campaign and stood in competition with AA, and many simply refused to accept the notion of a woman in such a role.

In the beginning, Bill Wilson and Dr. Bob Smith served as members of NCEA's advisory board and readily assented to having their names printed on the council's letterhead and promotional materials. Mindful of AA's central tenet of anonymity, they reasoned that the exposure would be acceptable because they weren't explicitly identified as alcoholics and members of AA. But Mann's press release announcing the NCEA's debut in October 1944 did exactly that: it listed Wilson and Smith as "founder and co-founder of Alcoholics Anonymous." Later, in 1946, when Yale was to begin reducing its funding of NCEA, because the plan had been for the council to become self-supporting after two years, Mann sent out a fundraising letter with AA mentioned all through it, identifying herself as a member and, again, AA's cofounders as members of the board.

AA members received the letter and became confused and concerned that it was AA doing the soliciting. Angry letters and phone calls poured into AA's central offices in New York, and the cofounders were taken aback by the outcry. Mann and her organization were getting results, bringing new members into AA with every public appearance, every mention in the media. Now ten years old, the fellowship was growing like never before, turning into the massive alcoholic-saving force Wilson had envisioned in its early days, when he'd gone to Rockefeller begging for backing. But the revolt by members was so fierce, he and Smith acquiesced, resigned from the board, and pulled their names from all NCEA materials.

Mann eventually bowed to the uproar as well. After two years of touring the country, with hundreds of media appearances, she agreed to stop identifying herself as a member of AA. She continued to confess to being a recovered alcoholic, but she stopped saying precisely how she'd recovered.

But the message never really changed, and one of the core planks of her campaign—the establishment of local operating committees—was undeniably linked to AA, albeit covertly.

Mann envisioned a nationwide network of alcoholism advocacy groups in communities across the United States and North America, each with a five-point plan to follow: "1) An intensive plan of education in their own area. 2) Establishment of an Alcoholic Information Center. 3) Procurement of hospital beds in general hospitals for the treatment of acute cases. 4) Establishment of a diagnostic and treatment clinic. 5) Establishment of rest centers for long-term care, at low cost or free if necessary." These local organizing committees proliferated quickly. At the end of 1945, the NCEA had five affiliates, including Washington, DC; Boston; Minneapolis; and Santa Barbara. By 1948, that number had grown to thirty-nine, several of which were statewide (Utah, Rhode Island, Pennsylvania).

Despite the mention of "hospitals" and "diagnostic and treatment clinic" and "rest centers for long-term care" in the five-point plan, the true day-to-day mission of these Alcoholic Information Centers was to get people into AA. The centers were staffed by members of AA and their friends and family, and when alcoholics or their loved ones would call asking for help, they would direct them to local meetings or put them in contact with area AA members.

A written exchange between one of Mann's top assistants and an AA member inquiring about establishing a local office in South Carolina is telling of both the NCEA's mission to promote AA and the ways in which it sought to obscure that mission. In his letter, the would-be local committee organizer seemed to have a hunch that it was important to keep an arm's length distance from AA, writing that he intended to found the committee "only as a citizen of Charleston and not as an AA member and will not make known my connection with AA." The assistant replied: "Most of the National Committee are members of [AA], and are most anxious that nothing ever be done by us or our organization that will disturb or hinder local AA Groups in their work of rehabilitation," adding that "any AA member who goes on one of these committees should do it in his own personal capacity as a citizen. His anonymity should be guarded and his membership in AA should never be publicized." Then in the next paragraph, as the assistant described the committee's primary functions, the staffer wrote that their "priority is to aid AA."

Years later, at an annual meeting of Mann's group, Wilson himself candidly explained and lauded the role her campaign played in AA's growth and success. "Without our friends, not only could we have not existed in the first place but we could not have grown," he said, adding "without any reservation" that Mann's operation

> has been responsible for making more friends for Alcoholics Anonymous and of doing a wider service in educating the world on the gravity of this malady and what can be done about it than any other single agency.
>
> And that it was designed to do those things for alcoholism which AA could not, and did not wish to do. . . . There is a close working relationship between the loosely knit fellowship of AA and the formal organization of [NCEA].

The Minnesota Model

While Yale University—despite its odd affiliation with AA via Mann's campaign—was using sound scientific methods to develop a model treatment program it hoped would become a national system for treating alcoholism, another treatment system was being created, not by doctors and scientists and institutional capital but by a drunk whose sobriety and life's mission began with a borrowed dime.

In 1939 Pat Cronin, a heavy drinker in Minneapolis, read a review in *Time* of a new book called *Alcoholics Anonymous* and asked his sister for ten cents so he could check it out from the library. Inside he found an address, so he wrote a letter on August 9, 1940, to AA's central office asking if there were "alumnae" in his area, signing it, "Cynically yours." Bill Wilson's personal secretary responded: no, there weren't, but there was a new group in Chicago, and she would pass his contact info on to them. Soon two recovering alcoholics from the Windy City arrived, both in town for a college football game of Minnesota versus Michigan. After the game, they paid a visit to Cronin, who was nursing a quart of Old Grand-Dad. They told Cronin how the program works, and Cronin felt he'd finally found something that might save him. But he asked, "What will I do when you leave?" As if in answer, snow came dumping down, socking the two visitors in for four days, during which they talked about the program nonstop. The snow cleared, the men left, and Cronin never drank again.

Cronin started an AA group and went around visiting drunk tanks and hospitals in the Twin Cities, looking for alcoholics to help. City social workers took notice. For some time they had been observing a correlation between alcohol abuse and financial destitution. One of the families they'd been working with, which had been on and off welfare rolls for more than ten years, no longer needed help because the father was now employed and supporting his wife and kids. They investigated and found that the man had sobered up through AA. They conducted a yearlong study in which they provided specialized service to families with alcoholic fathers, and they found that they could save money by doing this. They proposed establishing a clinic for the treatment of alcoholics.

They scouted the Twin Cities and found a spot they thought would be perfect. But then a newspaper article about their efforts appeared with the headline CITY BUYS A DORMITORY FOR DRUNKS. This sparked protests from the residential neighborhood around the building where they proposed to establish their treatment facility. The head of a local rescue mission offered to relocate the facility on property the mission owned in Medicine Lake known as Mission Hills. The facility opened in October 1948. It moved in and out of various buildings before settling in an old potato warehouse. The group turned it into a treatment center and called it Pioneer House.

Cronin came on staff as a counselor, though he had no formal training, just his experience in AA. Concerned that his new role could violate AA tradition, Cronin traveled to New York and consulted with Bill Wilson, who encouraged him to pursue the position, reasoning that his pay would be for his work as a social worker and not as a member of AA. Ironically, Cronin's job was very similar to the one Wilson, AA's cofounder, had been offered years earlier by Charles Towns but which other early AA members had urged him not to take.

Cronin and his new employers at Pioneer House wanted to hire more recovering alcoholics, believing they were best suited to help other alcoholics because of their firsthand experience with alcoholism. This experience, they believed, was more valuable than higher education. The problem was that the Minnesota Civil Service Commission required counselors to have at least a master's degree. So Cronin and his affiliates lobbied to change this, to create a new job category, "alcoholic counselors." When Minnesota's then-governor Elmer Anderson first heard this term, he laughed out loud.

The proposed new job title would require just two years of sobriety and a high school diploma. In lobbying for this new category, proponents for the treatment center also pushed for these new workers to earn the same salaries as counselors with graduate degrees in social work, which of course spurred resentment among social workers. The AA community also pushed back, arguing that it was a professionalization of AA and a violation of its traditions.

But Cronin and his colleagues prevailed, and now it was happening: AA was becoming professionalized. Recovered alcoholics provided "street education" to the few medical and psychology professionals who worked on staff at the treatment center and, according to a self-published history of the Pioneer House and the other treatment centers that followed, "AA and AA members became our model, our consultants and our advisory board."

"The primary influence that shaped Pioneer House was AA," wrote William White in *Slaying the Dragon: The History of Addiction Treatment and Recovery in America*. When new patients checked in, they received a copy of the Big Book, and while in treatment they worked on the first five of the Twelve Steps—they wouldn't be allowed to leave until they completed this admission of past wrongs to God and another person. In his work at the facility, Cronin emphasized spiritual transformation. He would ask his patients to row out to the middle of Medicine Lake, preferably at dawn, and drift peacefully on the water, awaiting divine inspiration and insight.

This odd strategy seemed to be working. In its first year, the center treated more than two hundred alcoholics, only twenty-two of whom returned after relapses. Four counselors and a director staffed the facility. Cronin would actively recruit patients, paying visits to the welfare department, municipal courts, and probation office. They also looked for ways to expand, to reach beyond skid-row drunks and help alcoholics who had solid jobs but were spiraling downward. To lay the groundwork for such an effort, they received $11,000 in donations from the Catholic diocese and area business leaders. In need of more space for this expansion, they found a farm in Center City, Minnesota, with 217 acres and a seventeen-room farmhouse and, with money from the Coyle Foundation, a Midwestern charity, they purchased it. It was known as Hazelden, after a woman named Hazel who had lived at the farm previously. As was the case at the Pioneer House, patients received a course of remedy that consisted almost exclusively of AA tenets—a thorough working of steps one through five—and this method would come to be known as the "Minnesota Model," the standard for alcoholism treatment in America.

Hazelden's treatment program rested on eleven tenets:

1. Alcoholism is a primary disease.
2. It's progressive.
3. It's incurable.
4. Motivation for recovery is not a predictor of success.
5. Treatment includes physical, psychological, social, and spiritual dimensions.
6. Treatment requires an environment of dignity and respect.
7. Alcoholics are susceptible to abuse of drugs.
8. Chemical dependency is best treated by a multidisciplinary team.
9. A focal point for treatment is an assigned primary counselor of the same sex.
10. Successful treatment includes orientation to AA.
11. Ongoing sobriety depends on continued participation in AA.

A member of AA served as its first general manager, and two other members of AA came on staff as its counselors. One of these men had undergone treatment himself at the facility, a questionable move that marked the beginning of what would become common practice decades later when alcoholism treatment would evolve into a booming industry. Patients were expected to "practice responsible behavior, attend the lectures on the Steps, associate and talk with other patients, and make their beds," according to Hazelden's written rules. There was some medical care—medicine, vitamin B shots, yeast tablets, and a placebo. But mostly patients were "given an intense indoctrination into the AA program," White observed.

The cost for treatment at Hazelden was $100 for the first week and $85 for each week thereafter. Though the goal was to treat the professional class, many of the early patients were destitute alcoholics from the Twin Cities whose fees were covered by a St. Paul charity. On average, there were between four and seven patients in residence on any given day, with an average length of stay of five days, but in time the program amassed more capital, constructed more buildings, and expanded. Staff beefed up after-care, established an alumni network that held meetings and helped conduct follow-ups, and established a halfway house—Fellowship House—to help patients reintegrate into day-to-day life. They opened a women's program on a three-hundred-acre estate near White Bear Lake in 1956 and named it Dia Linn (Gaelic for "God be with us"). This new center offered a four-week program based on a belief that it was more difficult to treat women.

Patrick Butler, who had purchased the farm that housed the Hazelden treatment center, had a vision of using Hazelden as a model that could be replicated at similar facilities across the country. Hazelden leaders traveled to conferences to share their efforts and successes. And some alumni of the Minnesota programs spread the word as they continued their newfound sobriety (by 1986, Hazelden's alumni association would boast more than five thousand members). Marty Mann's group was also an early champion, embracing the Minnesota Model as a local treatment approach promoted by the NCEA's local committees.

Hazelden staff members were invited to be consultants in other communities, and the requests so grew in number that they began holding regular training sessions in Center City. In 1960, the center received visitors from twenty-six states, five Canadian provinces, and four European countries. One attendee described the trip as being like "a pilgrim going to Mecca."

"The model got passed" along to other communities, White wrote, "not only because of Hazelden's reputation, but because of the infectious enthusiasm that permeated the place. There was no concern about giving away proprietary secrets: everything they had was yours for the asking. What you caught was the sense of being part of a social movement to spread alcohol treatment."

Jellinek's Doodle

As the Minnesota Model was beginning to emerge in the late 1940s, Marty Mann's campaign rolled on. She traveled tens of thousands of miles and reached millions through newspaper and magazine articles, radio and newsreel reports, and even movies. But all the while the tension with her benefactors at Yale increased. The fundamental conflicts between her mission and Yale's were becoming more and more clear. "Whereas Haggard and those associated with him at the Yale Center were concerned with bringing about a fundamental change in the way alcohol and the many problems associated with that substance were viewed," wrote Johnson, "Marty Mann was solely interested in popularizing the concept of alcoholism as a disease."

Yale had offered to fund Mann's campaign for two years, after which the NCEA was to become self-funding. But Mann struggled to raise funds, and she spent the bulk of her time spreading the story of alcoholism as a disease and AA as its cure. She even scolded Haggard and others at Yale for not staying on message—*her* message. In a letter to the Ivy League scientist, written in response to materials from Yale referring to a "drinking habit," she warned him that "if you accept the term 'drinking habit,' you are laid open to the admission that any habit can be overcome by will-power alone and furthermore, that all habit is something willfully or at least willingly entered into by its possessor, which can be equally willingly broken 'if he will only try' or even more, 'if he will only see the evils of his ways and promise reform.'"

At the same time that she doubted the efficacy of a scientific approach to treating alcoholism and rankled at Haggard's and his colleagues' openness to the obvious fact that drinking problems manifest themselves in a variety of ways, with differing levels of severity, she urged her backers at Yale to provide more scientific proof to support the uniform picture of alcoholism as a disease that she was painting in her travels around the country. In a letter to Haggard in August 1948, she wrote, "Incidentally, I want to add here, that I feel strongly the need for more physiological research under the Yale plan. I get more questions on that than any other phase of our work excepting on how can *we* help *them* to *do* something."

She even went so far as to help manufacture evidence to back up her claims. Early on, she gave Jellinek data from a survey AA members had conducted of themselves in the *Grapevine*, AA's official newsletter and journal (after editing out some of the responses herself). She asked him to analyze it, to find in the numbers a scientific model for alcoholism. "The exact origins of the *Grapevine* survey are unknown," wrote sociologist Ron Roizen. "My hunch is that once Marty Mann embarked on marketing the disease concept to the American public she encountered questions about the concept she could not adequately address. It's likely, moreover, that when Mann called for backup at the Yale group its scientists had little help to offer."

Jellinek was the only one interested in the data, and even he knew it was tainted. As he was analyzing it, his colleagues derisively referred to his project as "Jellinek's doodle."

He produced two articles from the findings. In the first, published in 1946, he framed his findings with a slew of caveats. "I have undertaken this work with great interest but also with many misgivings," he wrote. "Statistical thinking should not begin after a survey or an experiment has been completed but should enter into the first plans for obtaining the data."

He added: "Another limitation is inherent in the small number of completed questionnaires. While 158 members of Alcoholics Anonymous filled in the forms, only 98 questionnaires of male alcoholics could be used." Here he placed an asterisk alerting the reader to a footnote: "Fifteen questionnaires were returned by female alcoholics and these were excluded from the analysis because on the one hand the number was too small to be analyzed separately, and on the other hand because the data differed so greatly for the two sexes that merging the data was inadvisable." He added that seventeen had filled out the forms incorrectly, answering yes or no instead of providing dates, and one AA group pooled its responses and averaged them.

"In view of the methodological deficiencies and numerical limitations a detailed analysis of this material may not seem justified," he admitted, but stressed that "the material is so suggestive of future possibilities, however, that it would appear not only useful but practically imperative to submit the data to students of alcoholism."

As Roizen explained,

> First, Yale scientists hired a publicist to promote the disease concept. Then the concept turned out to lack good scientific legs. The publicist, in turn, launched her own survey study—in order to provide rudimentary data buttressing alcoholism's disease character. Next, a Yale scientist reluctantly agreed to analyze the data. He published two papers stemming from the data (1946 and 1952). In due course a chart showing alcoholism's symptom progression (in the 1952 paper) became widely distributed within the alcoholism movement.

Indeed, "Jellinek's doodle" became, in the words of one of Roizen's colleagues, fellow sociologist Robin Room, "the most widely diffused artifact of the alcoholism movement's disease concept."

"Throttled to Death by Yale"

Haggard and his colleagues at Yale were finding that they were getting more than they'd bargained for by taking on Mann's mission. She was generating more publicity than they could've imagined, but it was promoting an image of alcoholism that they didn't subscribe to, and it undermined their own efforts to develop scientific approaches to treating the disorder.

On the plus side, though, her work was sparking meaningful policy discussions and actions at the state and local levels across the country. As a direct result of her campaign, twenty-two states established alcoholism divisions in their governments, and Massachusetts and Connecticut started a network of alcoholism clinics. In 1947, Congress passed the Alcoholic Rehabilitation Act, which established treatment clinics in Washington, DC, but the funds for the effort weren't made available until 1966. Then–US congressman Lyndon Johnson had become a member of the NCEA in 1948, through its local organizing committee in Austin, Texas, and he would remain a powerful card-carrying member through the remainder of his political career.

Even religious institutions, which had been the driving force behind Prohibition, began to embrace a medical concept of alcoholism: in 1946, the General Assembly of the Presbyterian Church officially recognized alcoholism as a disease, and in 1947, the now defunct Federal Council of Churches did the same.

Watching all this unfold from New Haven, Haggard and Jellinek were pleased at the progress. They were not happy, however, that Mann couldn't expand these successes into the fundraising arena. Yale's patience was growing thin, and Mann desperately tried to find new donors. In March 1948, she reached out as others before her had to Rockefeller, writing to the director of the Rockefeller Brothers Fund, asking for money to expand operations. "The very nature of our work calls for constant expansion," she said in her request. She provided financial statements that showed that the committee had $13,328 on hand, after a year in which it had spent $55,299. For the coming year, 1948, it projected expenses of $80,000. It had only $58,500 pledged from various sources, including $20,000 from Yale.

Rockefeller declined to offer support. In August 1948, Mann wrote Haggard begging for more money: "I am, as you must know, deeply concerned about the future of the Committee. I do not see how we can be allowed to fail, for we are in effect, the public arm of all this work. And the work—all of it—MUST go on."

But soon thereafter, Haggard stepped away from the alcohol program he had established to become a full-time fundraiser for Yale. Sociologist Selden Bacon, who had come into a leadership position at Yale's alcohol project after it struck a partnership with Mann, took Haggard's place as director of the Yale center.

Bacon had long harbored doubts about Mann's activities and in particular had rejected Mann's assertion that AA is the only surefire cure for alcoholism. In fact, he wasn't convinced that alcoholism is a disease—as a sociologist, he thought it more likely to be a behavioral disorder. "Although financial issues undoubtedly were critical, the real source of difficulty can probably be traced to Haggard's and Bacon's lack of sympathy for the propagandist character of Marty Mann's crusade," Bruce Holley Johnson wrote of the tensions between Mann and Yale. "In later years, Bacon generally referred to the National Committee and those associated with its work as the 'alcoholic cult.'"

His attitude reflected that of the greater Yale University community, which was growing uncomfortable with what it was seeing from the alcohol project, as expressed most visibly through Mann's relentless national campaign. This reached scandalous levels after the NCEA published a pamphlet called "My Daddy Didn't Do It" that told the story of a child who was alarmed by her father's drinking. It was fictional, and they gave the father the name Harry Brown and a career as a banker who'd graduated from Yale. As it turns out, there were actually several Yale alumni named Harry Brown who'd gone into banking, and they and their friends and family fired off complaints to Yale.

In early 1949, Mann bore down on fundraising efforts. In May of that year, the NCEA launched a campaign called A-Day (A for alcoholism). Everyone in New York who drank would be asked to give at least the price of one drink toward furthering the work of the committee. They distributed to hotels, restaurants, nightclubs, and bars throughout the city posters, flyers and canisters that read YOU CAN DRINK. HELP THE ALCOHOLIC WHO CAN'T. ALCOHOLISM IS A DISEASE. As part of this campaign, Mann appeared on the popular *The Margaret Arlen Show*, broadcast nationally on the radio, declaring that alcoholism is a disease and urging alcoholics to go to AA. The campaign raised only enough to pay for the posters and canisters. "It was like pushing a boulder up a hill with your nose," she would later say of her failed efforts to raise sufficient funds.

The stress wore Mann down. "The business of putting on a big campaign is fabulous, and I wouldn't recommend it to a feeble-minded dog!" she wrote to a friend. "I don't know whether I'm coming or going and my head feels like a punching bag." To another she complained, "I'm afraid we have created almost a Frankenstein monster and my only worry is to keep it from consuming me before we can get adequate hands to control it." She was diagnosed with cancer, and for much of 1949 she lay in a hospital bed. Piles of get-well cards came pouring in.

In June 1949, still recuperating, she wrote Bill and Lois Wilson of the dire straits her committee faced, stating that a split with Yale was imminent, lamenting, "So this is it, Bill. Too bad. Too bad." Wilson replied that he found the news "terribly dispiriting to me. Yes, and more. It was devastating, because I understand, better than some, how much of your blood and courage has gone into the Committee. As one who has made an expenditure of this kind himself, I find it quite impossible to picture such a disappointment.

"Then I read your footnote," he continued, "and there between the lines, I could see you at your best even though enduring the worst. Somehow I could see you rising, Phoenix-like, from the ashes of the great flame you kindle: a flame whose warmth will be felt by many a generation of our brothers and sisters."

At the bottom of the letter, Lois wrote, "Many AA's don't understand how much you've helped the public to understand."

At the time, the committee's account had dwindled to $373.57.

Mann again was offered a chance to replenish her coffers, but the potential revenue stream came from a source that she found distasteful. In October of that year, Bacon of Yale wrote Franklin Houston, one of Mann's top assistants and friends, urging him to schedule a visit with "Coors in Denver, since Coors is not only interested in the National Committee, but is particularly interested in the financial support of the entire Yale plan. I think you should understand this and some of the other conversations that have been held with Mr. Coors before discussing the situation with him."

Houston demurred, saying the NCEA had a policy of not accepting money from alcohol concerns. (During a later speech at NYU, Mann appeared to regret this decision. "We have not got millions of dollars," she admitted, "and

I am afraid we are not likely to have them in the immediate future, because we have cut ourselves off, deliberately, from potential sources of income which might have supplied just that.")

When Mann's group balked at the Coors gambit, the tensions with Yale came to a head at a meeting of the committee's board in December 1949, where, in Mann's words, "all hell broke loose." Mann sat silently as Bacon railed about her undermining the mission of Yale and its Program on Alcohol. "They questioned everything," she wrote, "starting at the budget itself, and going from there to the repayment of old debts and the schedule for that, up to and at great length about the true functions of NCEA"—to serve the Yale plan. She called it a "knock-down-and-drag-out fight. I never spoke, and thank God I left the room during the discussion."

Bacon spoke at length about the "two underlying philosophies" of Yale and the committee, referring to her message of alcoholism as a unitary disease for which the only cure is AA, versus Yale's position—rooted in science—that problem drinking is the result of an array of disorders that require a variety of treatment approaches. That's when Mann left the room for a while, retreating farther and farther down the hall to move out of earshot.

The official minutes from the meeting include a memorandum from Bacon saying that the committee had become international in scope and had as such outgrown the appropriateness of being attached to a single university department—that it was outside the university's mission of undergraduate and graduate education and of research. He stated that the committee had also interfered with the university and the Yale Plan's ability to raise funds of its own. "The University is always fearful that its friends and supporters may feel that by giving to the National Committee they have contributed to Yale," he explained.

The next day, Haggard called from New Haven and yelled at Mann, telling her she should have her "irresponsible big-talking board members" take over if they want. And so she agreed to break ties. At the NCEA's next board meeting two weeks later, the board members crafted an announcement of the split, stating that the relationship had become "increasingly untenable" and the faculty and staff at the university were "increasingly uncomfortable" with being pulled into a national campaign for policy and health.

Afterward, Mann wrote in a letter to a friend that she felt relieved not to be "throttled to death by Yale—or perhaps smothered is a better word." But now she sat at the head of a wildly successful national organization, with a network of dozens of regional offices full of staffers and volunteers—many of them members of AA working anonymously, all eager to pound into the American mind the belief that alcoholism is a disease and AA is the cure—but with no budget and no esteemed institution of science on which to hang her unproven claim.

3 | 1953-1970: DRUNK WITH POWER

Lobbyists Anonymous

In her final annual report to Yale in late 1949, Marty Mann had bragged of her organization's successes—the dozens of states that had considered legislation on alcoholism, the media triumphs—but warned that they weren't enough. She lacked the funds to adequately continue the job. "A budget of $50,000 or even $60,000 is not sufficient to meet the need," she wrote. "Nor is the National Committee justified in asking men and women to give their physical and emotional strength, their abilities and their experience to full time work at the financial sacrifice that makes such a budget necessary. It is imperative that financial support far more generous than in past years be forthcoming. The alternative is rather shocking to consider."

But at the beginning of the 1950s, the "alternative" had become reality. Operating under a new name, the National Council on Alcoholism (NCA) received a few donations. Silent film star Mary Pickford became a friend of Mann's and gave occasional contributions. But at every turn, Mann's campaign teetered on the brink of financial collapse. At one point her council received an anonymous donation of $10,000. That sum was not nearly enough.

In 1953 Mann laid off staff and replaced them with volunteers. This not only hampered the council's effectiveness but also further defined it as a propaganda vessel for AA because the council's central offices in New York and in local offices across the country were invariably staffed by members of AA and their loved ones. These local affiliates were particularly powerful. They'd contact public officials at all levels of power—from county health departments all the way up to governors' offices and members of Congress, social workers, civic and religious organizations, newspaper editorial boards, and the regular folks they'd interact with every day—and spread AA gospel through plain old word of mouth. But under AA's tradition of anonymity, they did so without disclosing their affiliation and so became, in effect, a vast lobbying organization that kept secret the concern for which they lobbied.

Years earlier, under pressure from fellow members of AA, Bill Wilson and Robert Smith had removed themselves from the board of Mann's organization, and Mann had stopped identifying herself as a member of AA. But many in the public continued to equate her with AA. People would often hear Mann on the radio or read about her in the newspaper and address correspondence to her, mailing their letters to AA's central office instead of hers. In a letter to a friend, Mann joked, "One of the girls down there [at AA] complained to me the other day that she was a little tired of acting as my secretary! And I can't really blame her when I see how much mail addressed to me goes to them."

More often, people would contact the NCA seeking help for their drinking problems or for their friends and family. These inquiries were often answered by Mann's assistant, Julliette Clark, who would openly identify herself as "an AA member" and tell them how to find local meetings. A man writing from Middletown, California, wrote that he had gotten sober on his own and wanted to help a few of his friends quit drinking as well. Clark replied, "Most people are unable to [get sober] without assistance, which they should be encouraged to find. If there is an AA Group in your town, and you are not already familiar with the work the members do, you may wish to get in touch with them and learn how their program works, and encourage those people who are having trouble gaining sobriety to try the AA Program."

Clark would push AA's concept of the disease of alcoholism, the idea that one had to continue drinking until life got so intolerable that one was ready to accept the cure of abstinence, God, and AA. To a woman in New York seeking help for her sister, she wrote, "If your sister is as yet unwilling even to try A.A., there is little they can do until she, herself, is willing to listen."

But while Mann and her associates were willing to help individuals in need, their mission was to convince a nation that such individuals were worth helping, that they could be helped, and that AA offered a cure. Amid their financial struggles, completion of this mission seemed impossibly far away.

During this dark stretch, at a point when it seemed it all would come crashing down in financial ruin, Mann made a prediction to one of her top assistants: "There is a rich drunk out there somewhere who will get sober and help us."

"You Have the Money Now"

Enter R. Brinkley Smithers, son of a founder of IBM and grandson of a prominent banker who headed a Wall Street investment firm. Born into this wealth in the wake of the tragic death of an older brother who was just four years old, Smithers seemed destined to a charmed life. "Having eased his parents' grief over the loss of their first child," *Town & Country* magazine wrote in a profile of him, "little Brinkley could, from the beginning, do no wrong."

He grew up on a Long Island estate and passed the time hunting and fishing. He was turned down by Princeton but accepted into Johns Hopkins's premed program. There he had his first martini, which, to his delight, banished his shyness and filled him with confidence. It was the height of Prohibition, but he struck a deal with a chemistry professor to partake of the lab's alcohol supply. He specialized in making gin—a gallon of ethanol, a gallon of water, some glycerin, and a few drops of juniper essence or apricot drops.

He made it two years at Johns Hopkins before his dad pulled him out, scolding him for not knowing "where the country club quits and college begins." He was put to work at the family's Wall Street firm but was promptly arrested for driving drunk, after which his father took him for a round of golf and a man-to-man talk about booze, but it had little effect.

Brink, as his friends and family called him, threw himself into the Roaring Twenties. He'd summer at the Long Island shore, attend debutante balls during the social season, and then bask in the winter sun in Palm Beach. All around him people were drinking hard; compared to them, he seemed normal. He didn't cause scenes or land in jail, so he slipped through with his drinking and did well enough at the New York firm to be promoted to run it. In that role, he thrived, making the company's largest sale to date—business machines for the newly created Social Security Administration.

But he preferred drinking to working, so at thirty he retired to a farm in Maryland and, from there, would set out on hunting expeditions in South Carolina, Long Island, and Peru. Then after a boozy round of golf at Congressional Country Club in Bethesda, he rear-ended a car. With good lawyers, he got the charges dropped, but things kept getting worse. He'd drink in secret, down booze before breakfast, and escape to New York for epic binges. On those days, he'd start the day with two whiskey sours and some toast and coffee, drive to the city, leave his suitcase at Towns Hospital, where Bill Wilson had his spiritual experience and the first seeds of AA had been sown, and go drinking around the city until a little after midnight. Then he'd check himself in to the hospital, availing himself of its tapering-off regimen of a drink an hour, then one every two hours, diminishing for five days. Smithers did this more than fifty times in the late 1940s and early '50s.

In 1952, his dad died. Smithers was named as executor of his father's estate, and he founded Christopher D. Smithers Foundation in his honor. Now in his late forties, the weight of the responsibility for this philanthropic endeavor pressed on him, and he grew weary of his drinking. On one of his stays at Towns Hospital, despairing, he called an old employee of his whom he had fired for drinking on the job. The man had quit drinking, and Smithers hoped maybe his old employee could help him sober up, too. His friend introduced him to Yev Gardner, Marty Mann's top assistant at the NCA.

Gardner told Smithers his own story of struggle with alcoholism, which was remarkably similar to Smithers's. He explained to Smithers that they both suffered from a disease, and upon hearing this, something shifted inside Smithers. "Deep down, I had suspected this, that I was suffering from a disease that, for some reason or another, I was particularly susceptible to," he would later say, but it had always been little more than a hunch. Here was someone confirming it with a story—*his* story, the story of alcoholism as a disease. Instantly he felt relief, and for the first time in many years, hope.

But, he wondered, why had no one ever told him about this disease before? Why hadn't anyone launched a massive campaign to get the truth out about the disease of alcoholism?

Gardner replied that people were trying to do just that, that he was part of an organization striving to educate the public about alcoholism. He told Smithers about Yale's early support that had dried up and how the organization was now struggling just to get by. The group just didn't have the money, Gardner said, to properly carry out its mission.

Smithers, with a multimillion-dollar foundation under his command, replied, "Well, you have the money now."

Five Out of Ten Doctors Approve

Gardner introduced Smithers to Marty Mann, and the two met over a cup of tea in a Manhattan cafe. Mann asked if he'd be willing to serve on the NCA's board. He immediately agreed to act as treasurer, and in the coming years he would become president and chairman of the board. A powerful figure in the group for decades, he was candid about the council's relationship to AA, which he depicted as "the retail side," where the story of the disease of alcohol would be sold to the individual alcoholic, and the NCA as "the wholesale side," where the story would be sold to the nation.

His first contribution was $10,000 (the equivalent of $90,000 in 2017 dollars). One of his earliest initiatives as treasurer was to spearhead what he called the "big step-up," a fundraising campaign with a goal of boosting the NCA's annual income to $200,000 (the equivalent of $1.8 million in 2017 dollars). Smithers contributed a lot of his own money and in time would donate millions, both from his father's foundation and his own estate.

"From the beginning this man didn't just lend his name nor did he just sign checks," Mann would later say of her new benefactor. "He worked." For years he and Mann met for lunch a couple times a week in the restaurant at the luxurious Stanhope Hotel on Fifth Avenue overlooking Central Park and the Metropolitan Museum of Art, and he arranged for Mann to have a generous clothing allowance. "She's the queen, and I'm the king," Smithers would often say of their relationship.

In addition to money, what Mann needed in the early 1950s was what Bill Wilson had told her she'd need when she first came up with the idea to launch a national campaign: scientific backing. Having separated from Yale, she could no longer identify herself as a representative of the Ivy League institution and lean on its credibility. Mann and her staff continued trying to work with Yale faculty, seeking information and confirmation for the concept of alcoholism they were promoting. In the process, they sometimes stretched the boundaries of sound scientific practice. In one instance, an NCA staffer contacted a former Yale professor for permission to use an offhanded comment he'd uttered years earlier, that only 10 to 15 percent of alcoholics "were of the visible skid row type." The council's aim was to change the public perception of alcoholism as solely an affliction of bums, so this information would be helpful. The professor, Dr. Robert Straus, then at the University of Kentucky, replied, "I have been trying to recall just when and under what circumstances I might have made such an estimate. To my knowledge this factor has never been counted or measured and any statistic must necessarily be guesses." But, he added, "If you feel that this would have any value, you may quote this as a personal opinion."

On another occasion the same staffer wrote Selden Bacon at Yale for permission to quote an article in which he wrote that three out of four alcoholics are between the ages of twenty-five and fifty-five. "I suppose it's alright for you to quote the age-range figure," Bacon replied.

> Nobody knows, and this sounds just as worthwhile as many other statements which purport to be factual. I think the statement would be somewhat better if it started with 'probably,' but this might so weaken it for your purposes that you would prefer to have it as in your letter. So, go ahead and, if anybody challenges it, we'll just counter-challenge them to produce a better figure.

But amping up offhand, unproven comments from distinguished university faculty wasn't sufficient for the NCA's purposes. It needed a concise, powerful confirmation for what it believed to be true, and it sought this validation from the American Medical Association. If it could get the AMA to declare that alcoholism is a disease, the campaign would move to solid ground.

The effort to procure the AMA's endorsement began during Mann's organization's last year of affiliation with Yale. Dr. Milton Potter, a recovering alcoholic and doctor from Buffalo, established the Western New York Committee for Education on Alcoholism during a 1949 meeting in Mann's office, with the specific goal of getting the AMA to recognize alcoholism as a disease. Potter worked closely with Ruth Fox, medical director at the NCA, as well as another Buffalo physician named Marvin Block, who, as a professor of medicine at the State University of New York at Buffalo, was well connected to local, state, and national medical societies. Block and Potter had gone to medical school together, and after Potter had gotten sober, Block approached him for help with a patient who was struggling with drinking. Block began taking on more and more alcoholic patients until his practice focused almost entirely on that area, and he began working with Potter to broaden acceptance in the medical community of the notion of alcoholism as an illness. Block became a board member of the NCA. He would later tell an interviewer that he was driven by ambition.

He wanted to achieve a national reputation as an authority in the field of alcoholism, to be recognized as a key figure in the medicalization of the condition.

For Block, the key to this effort lay in the Twelve Steps of AA. "Perhaps the most effective treatment in the rehabilitation of the alcoholic is a philosophy of living which is compatible with the individual and his family, an absorbing faith in himself which comes only after he has learned to understand himself, and a close association with others whose experiences parallel his own," he would write. "The physician's cooperation with Alcoholics Anonymous is one way of obtaining these things for his patient."

In short order, Block and Potter created a pilot project of a treatment facility program within a local hospital, secured a grant from the New York Department of Mental Hygiene to create a rehabilitation center, and received another grant from the Buffalo Council of Social Agencies to establish an alcoholism information center that, according to its mission statement, worked in "close liaison with the local groups of Alcoholics Anonymous . . . and many individuals are referred to that fellowship for long range rehabilitation." With these efforts underway, the two New York doctors persuaded the New York State Medical Society to establish a subcommittee on alcoholism, a significant first step toward their goal of getting the AMA to designate alcoholism as a disease.

There was precedent for this: in 1950, the World Health Organization had formed a committee on alcoholism and hired Bunky Jellinek, who had left Yale after Howard Haggard stepped away from his alcohol project to concentrate on fundraising. After several months of work, Jellinek wrote a report and resolution defining alcoholism as "a chronic behavior disorder manifested by repeated drinking of alcoholic beverages in excess of dietary and social uses of the community and to an extent that interferes with the drinker's health or his social and economic functioning." Though the resolution didn't define alcoholism specifically as a disease, it was still a formal declaration about problem drinking issued by a widely respected health organization, and this moved the problem from being an issue of morality to one of medicine and health care.

Block and Potter faced a steep challenge. In the United States, most medical professionals remained leery of problem drinkers and would rarely treat them, because heavy drinking was still seen as a moral issue. Most hospitals turned away drunks. And when *Alcoholics Anonymous*, AA's Big Book, came out in 1939, the AMA's journal had called it "a curious combination of organizing propaganda and religious exhortation. It is in no sense a scientific book" and of "no scientific merit or interest."

At the AMA's 1950 convention in San Francisco, Block and Potter led the New York delegation to introduce a resolution to establish a committee on alcoholism. The measure failed on a 40–56 vote. They reintroduced it, and it tanked again. They lobbied for the better part of the next year, and in June 1951 they won a narrow approval, though the AMA refused to appropriate any funds for it and the committee disbanded. Block and Potter redoubled their campaign, focusing on the AMA's burgeoning efforts to address issues of mental health. In 1952, the AMA established a Council on Mental Health, and in early 1954, the council created a Committee on Alcoholism, headed by Block, which developed an ambitious eighteen-point program. The committee's goals included establishing alcoholism committees in all county medical societies, promoting curricula on alcoholism in medical schools, providing postgraduate training courses, establishing medical terminology on alcoholism, persuading insurance companies to recognize and cover alcoholism, establishing minimal standards of treatment, getting state health departments to develop policies on alcoholism, encouraging research in physiological and pathological aspects of alcoholism, developing adequate statistics on alcoholism, and consulting on the proper use of drugs in treatment.

Despite these calls for medical approaches, several of the points on the committee's platform betrayed the true nature of the treatment it was promoting. One telling phrase was to "encourage the use of 'recovered' instead of 'cured'"—a clear nod to AA's belief that alcoholics are forever afflicted. More overtly, the committee called for "working closely with community groups, especially AA," and promoting establishment of local NCA committees, referring to Mann's group, the anonymous lobbying wing of AA.

It became clear, however, that the committee lacked support in the AMA to get alcoholism designated as a disease, so its members focused on a campaign for a resolution calling for hospitals to admit and treat problem drinkers. At the time, problem drinking was handled primarily as a criminal justice issue—severe drunks, to the extent they were dealt with at all, were thrown in jail for a night to sober up or sent to prisons for the criminally insane for longer stretches. If they could be admitted to hospitals instead, the committee reasoned, they could receive drugs to help stabilize them and a safe bed. In hospitals, they could also be more easily reached by members of AA, who would then lead them to the more long-term remedy offered by the Twelve Steps.

But even this required significant effort. Members of the committee, including Block, wrote a series of articles on hospital treatment of alcoholics for the *Journal of the American Hospital Association*, which they reprinted as a treatment manual. The series coincided with an exhibit the committee made for AMA's 1955 convention, which displayed graphic representations of alcoholism's progression and offered stacks of brochures.

These efforts resulted in an official declaration titled, "Hospitalization of Patients with Alcoholism," which the AMA narrowly passed in 1956. But the resolution stopped short of calling alcoholism a disease, opting instead for "serious health problem." It referred to the alcoholic as "a sick individual" and alcoholics as "sick people."

"Technically, by voting to accept this resolution of the Council on Mental Health, the House of Delegates of the AMA did not officially endorse the position that 'alcoholism' (I.E. habitual drunkenness) is a disease," sociologist Johnson wrote in his dissertation.

> A resolution stating unequivocally that "alcoholism is a disease that merits serious concern of all members of the health professions" was eventually passed by the AMA, but this did not occur until the 1967 Clinical Session. However from November 1956 on, those who were attempting to gain acceptance for the idea that chronic drunkenness is in fact a disease or illness invariably argued that the AMA had declared that it is so.

After the 1956 resolution's passage, Jellinek ignored what the resolution actually said and declared that it "constitutes, of course, the formal acceptance of the disease conception of 'alcoholism' by the American medical profession as a whole." He conceded, however, that "this does not mean that acceptance among physicians is unanimous," adding: "physicians who do not view alcoholism as an illness are perhaps a minority but a rather sizable minority."

Reflecting on this slim but significant victory in a long campaign and sizing up the challenges that remained, Block wrote,

As with many other diseases that in the past were neglected, alcoholism will take its place, recognized by the physician as within his province—indeed, his duty—to treat with the same studiousness, devotion and interest he has given his other work. As with other illnesses, this interest will stimulate study and research. The history of medicine is highlighted with conquests of many serious diseases once the physician has accepted their challenge. The future may well see alcohol as one of them.

For Marty Mann, the vote was a fulsome, unanimous endorsement of the disease concept of alcoholism, even though it explicitly wasn't. For her and her PR campaign, what mattered was that America's premiere medical association had formally addressed the problem of alcoholism, and this was enough for her to seize onto and mold into her own message. For years to come she would often declare, "Alcoholism was the first disease they ever had to vote was a disease!"

"Let's Do It Together"

The NCA quickly surpassed its new treasurer R. Brinkley Smithers's goal of a $200,000 annual income. The nationwide network was becoming one of the most formidable PR operations of the twentieth century, and Mann ran her campaign with expert precision. She devised for her affiliates an impressive twenty-six-page publicity manual that spelled out exactly what constitutes news ("Almost anything the NCA affiliate does or says is of some news value, but it must be tied to an actual event. For example, NCA says 'Alcoholism is a disease.' This means nothing as news value unless it is said in a speech, at a meeting, in a statement, etc.") and detailed precisely how to find the appropriate news outlets, reporters, and editors to carry that news out into the world. The manual advised whom to include on mailing lists and under what circumstances to contact individual reporters directly as well as "the right publications and the proper departments."

By all measures the strategy was working. Johnson calculated a steep upturn in the amount of press coverage of alcoholism as a disease during the 1950s, a surge that exceeded the one Mann brought about when she began her organization in the 1940s. The NCA's local organizing committees were making inroads in state legislatures and executive branches across the country, the vast majority of which were considering and passing legislation to establish programs on alcoholism and treatment facilities that used the Minnesota Model of AA-based treatment. Every year the NCA would hold a multiday meeting of its affiliates, to which Mann invited leaders in the medical, civic, business, and religious communities. The proceedings, filled with hour after hour of presentations and panel discussions, were transcribed and preserved in bulky bound volumes.

Their 1957 annual meeting was held in an elegant hotel ballroom in Chicago, and it carried the theme "We Can Do It Together." Although the event's roster of presenters and attendees included people from a broad range of disciplines and backgrounds, suggesting a multifaceted approach to the problem of alcoholism, the message of each talk invariably repeated and reinforced AA's concept of alcoholism and its cure.

A speech called "How the Priest Can Help" presented by Rev. Joseph T. Manganese, professor of moral theology at St. Mary of the Lake Seminary, Mundelein, Illinois, concluded: "We shall provide the man with Alcoholics Anonymous literature and suggest that with a member he attend a few Alcoholics Anonymous meetings just to look around, if for nothing more. Ordinarily, today, if the alcoholic is serious in seeking recovery, he will become a member of Alcoholics Anonymous and faithfully follow their program."

The preacher warned that the alcoholic would first need to suffer mightily before this remedy would take hold. "After his first few meetings," Manganese said of the hypothetical drunk, "he may become convinced that he is not an alcoholic, since he has not 'hit as low a bottom' as many of the other members. This may start him off on another drinking spree. Before he becomes really convinced, he may leave to 'hit a lower bottom.'" Such a bottom could be quickened with help from the family, Manganese said, via what he called "'scudding a bottom,' such as the wife saying she'll leave him if he doesn't go to AA. And in such cases the clergy may help him 'accept the reasonableness and kindness of such 'cruelty.'"

Similarly, Dr. Granger E. Westberg, associate professor of religion and health at the University of Chicago, admitted the ineffectiveness of religion to help, in comparison to AA. In "The Pastor and the Alcoholic" he confessed that

the history of the past one hundred years indicates that the family minister, like the family doctor, was generally unsuccessful in his attempt to help the alcoholic. He was therefore overjoyed at learning of the success of the Alcoholics Anonymous movement. It is true that some of the more rigid clergy were upset by what they called the "poor theology" found in some of the statements by the AAs concerning God. But a great many more clergy saw in the twelve steps of AA the layman's remarkable insight into the traditional Christian way of salvation. . . . They were embarrassed to think that laymen had to teach them how to release the life-changing dynamic of the Christian faith.

The doctors who spoke demurred as well. In "A Physician's Viewpoint," Marvin A. Block, fresh off his success in cajoling the AMA into identifying alcoholics as "sick people," offered little true medical advice beyond sedating patients in the throes of drunkenness or DTs, hooking them to an IV, and filling them with vitamins to stabilize them. After that was done, he said it is always important to suggest the various facilities at the disposal of the family in connection with helping the individual. "I think that it is very important that the nurses know that there are such associations available," he explained. "Of course, Mrs. Mann mentioned Alcoholics Anonymous but then there are also many others. In almost every community in this country one doesn't have to go far to find one or another groups of AA. This can, of course, be a first line of defense."

Of the "many others" he offered no specifics.

Likewise, Dr. Ruth Fox, chief medical advisor for the NCA, gave a rundown of the kinds of medications that can help an alcoholic under the influence or going through withdrawal—thorazine, Equanil, Ultram—until "the third day, when they're up and walking around and they can talk with others who've been there awhile—'old-timers'—who can introduce them to AA."

But most telling was a talk by William C. Menninger, cofounder of the Menninger Foundation in Topeka, an internationally renowned pioneer in the treatment of behavioral disorders. This towering figure of twentieth-century psychiatry spent the entirety of his talk lamenting the inadequacy of his field in addressing the problem of alcoholism and conceding that "AA has been far more effective in helping thousands of people than has psychiatry."

Yet, despite all the pro-AA rallying calls, that same year, the NCA commissioned an audit of itself, an assessment of its operation's strengths and weaknesses, and the resultant report, known as the Franklin Report, after its author, Paul Franklin, candidly addressed the committee's relationship to AA. "There exists no other health problem in which a large, powerful, and extremely active lay group is already dealing effectively with it. This group, Alcoholics Anonymous, presents both an asset and a possible danger to the successful functioning of NCA," Franklin wrote. "It must be remembered that it has members in every city and town in the land, many of whom hold positions of authority, responsibility, and power. Not all AA members are favorably disposed toward the NCA, or indeed toward any group or individual outside of AA itself. When such members are in key spots, as they frequently are, this can slow or even stop our effective functioning."

Franklin added, "At present, the NCA family is primarily composed of recovered alcoholics who in turn largely limit their contacts and solicitation efforts to others who have had the disease. . . . It is essential that the Council acquire a more hopeful and expectant attitude as to the possibility of interesting non-alcoholics in its work and needs. Actually the agency has never adequately tested its ability to recruit outsiders as workers and givers."

Marty's Secrets

The late '50s and early '60s were high times for Marty Mann. Her partner, Priscilla Peck, was an art director for *Vogue*, and she was also sober through AA. They'd met early in Mann's sobriety, moved in together into a stylish Manhattan apartment, and bought a house on Fire Island in 1944, which they'd visit on weekends and feel at home in the gay and lesbian scene there. All her life she kept calling herself Mrs. Marty Mann, a shield to hide the fact that she was a lesbian, a secret she carefully guarded. Homosexuality was illegal then in New York and across the country, and she feared that if her sexual orientation were known, she would be looked on as a social deviant, and it would likely undermine her mission to make alcoholics socially acceptable and worthy of public sympathy.

Mann and Peck's apartment was adorned with modern art purchased from Peck's friend and famed gallery owner Betty Parsons, including a small early Jackson Pollack drip painting, *Number 15, 1949*, which is now owned by the Los Angeles County Museum of Art, and works by Mark Rothko and Clifford Still. Surprisingly, despite the demands of her job and her teetotaler status, Mann loved the nightlife. Tipping back virgin drinks—her favorite was a "horse's neck," ginger ale with a lemon twist—she'd often stay out until the wee morning hours, not showing up at the NCA's offices until nearly noon, and she and Peck always kept a full bar in their apartment for guests who didn't share their disease.

With her organization amply funded, Mann enjoyed a growing national profile. She'd even been approached by TV producers to develop a weekly show of stories about alcoholism. Called *Fork in the Road*, the series would be made "with the active cooperation and participation" of the National Council on Alcoholism, for which Mann would earn a consulting fee of $500 per episode. They hired screenwriters to develop pilot scripts, including one by William Inge, a playwright who had just won a Pulitzer Prize for his play *Picnic*. But the series never made it to production.

During this time, Mann had brief affairs with authors Carson McCullers and Jane Bowles, the former of whom apparently fell hard for Mann, penning to her several long love letters. Mann also, at some point during this period, relapsed into heavy drinking. The historical record of her slip is scant, because Mann worked hard to cover it up. What's known is that a young female member of AA who lived in Bronxville, with less than a year of sobriety, discovered her. The woman had heard much about Mann and longed to meet her. Other AA members encouraged her to go to Manhattan, so she did, unannounced. She found Mann drunk, the apartment a mess, dog shit all around. She loaded Mann and her dogs into her station wagon and took them home to Bronxville. Mann stayed there for a few days, refusing to go to AA, desperate to keep the episode a secret. Mann's closest AA friends, including Bill Wilson, quickly moved in to help, and they all agreed she should keep the episode secret. She couldn't risk revealing the truth: that the cure she preached was not as miraculous and absolute as she was leading the public to believe.

To this day, no one knows exactly when the relapse occurred, other than it happened at some point in the late '50s or early '60s. The only possible evidence that remains is a prescription for Antabuse Dr. Ruth Fox wrote out for Mann in 1964. Some of her speeches during this period often carried a dark tone that suggests her struggles. At a talk in San Francisco, for example, she said,

> The more I learn about alcoholism, the more frightening it becomes, let me tell you. This is a fearful disease that we've got. You and I know we haven't eliminated it out of ourselves. It's still there. We don't get

up here and say "I was an alcoholic," do we? I am an alcoholic. . . . One drink—that's all we need to start down that spiral into that lonely glass box again. And it is cunning, baffling, powerful. It does come back. And when you have a lot of problems over a period of time—a lot of stress and strain, a lot of crisis in your life—what is going to sustain you from taking that first drink?

"A Disease Is What the Medical Community Recognizes as Such"

To cement the notion that alcoholism is a disease, Brinkley Smithers commissioned Bunky Jellinek to write a book that would emphatically define it as such. Jellinek, ever energetic, took to the task with fervor, but in working on it he became more and more uncertain of the idea. His thinking about the matter had undergone a change during his time at the World Health Organization, where he'd worked closely with officials from other countries where the attitudes toward alcohol were different from those in the United States. In places such as Spain, Italy, and Japan, drinking was a more natural part of the culture. He began to see problem drinking not as a singular disease, like the one Mann was promoting, but a complex array of disorders that manifest themselves in many ways and for which there are numerous courses of remedy.

The resulting book, *The Disease Concept of Alcoholism*, published in 1960, reads in large part as an exercise in semantics, spending most of its two-hundred-plus pages prevaricating over nuances in the meaning of the words "disease" and "illness" and how they relate to alcoholism. In the end, its most emphatic statement is a confounding one: "It comes to this, that *a disease is what the medical community recognizes as such.*"

In other words, alcoholism is a disease if doctors say it is.

The scientific specifics that he does offer paint a picture quite different from the one-size-fits-all story of alcoholism that Mann and Smithers were pushing at the NCA. He argued that there are multiple "species" of problem drinkers: alpha (psychological dependence), beta (heavy drinking but no symptoms of addiction), gamma (psychological dependence that progresses to physical addiction), delta (steady, high-volume drinking that leads to physical dependence), and epsilon (binge drinker). He claimed that only two of these are true diseases—gamma and delta, because both involve physical addiction.

To put a finer point on it, he summarized: "There is not one alcoholism but a whole variety." This was at odds with the model promoted by Mann's campaign (including Smithers, the funder for Jellinek's book) and AA as a whole. "Members of Alcoholics Anonymous have naturally created the picture of alcoholism in their own image," he observed, the definition of which is spelled out in the "A Doctor's Opinion" preface to the Big Book, in which Dr. William Silkworth describes it as an allergy. Jellinek dismissed this allergy concept not as something rooted in medical science but as a metaphor. He was quick to state that there was usefulness in employing a metaphor in this way and stressed that he wasn't trying to "persuade Alcoholics Anonymous to abandon their conception. The figurative use of the term 'alcoholism is an allergy' is as good as or better than anything else for their purposes"—which was to motivate alcoholics to embrace abstinence as the only means of recovery—"as long as they do not wish to foist it upon students of alcoholism."

More sharply he wrote, "In spite of the respect and admiration to which Alcoholics Anonymous have a claim on account of their great achievements, there is every reason why the student of alcoholism should emancipate himself from accepting the exclusiveness of the picture of alcoholism as propounded by Alcoholics Anonymous."

But this is exactly what was happening—the picture of alcoholism was being painted entirely in the image of AA, by its members who were anonymously working on its behalf. "There are approximately 600,000 propagandists, namely, 200,000 members of Alcoholics Anonymous and their wives and children, who vigorously spread the idea that alcoholism is an illness," he wrote, "not through public speeches, nor through their numerous pamphlets, but rather by word of mouth in conversation with their many friends and business associates."

Jellinek feared that this would have grave consequences on the burgeoning field of alcoholism studies and treatment research—that if the field continued to follow the lead of AA, whose proponents uphold a definition of alcoholism as a singular disease, "the gains of the illness conception may be lost again," the gains being a move away from a moralistic and legalistic conception of the problem. "Generally, it may be said not only of the public at large but of the medical profession, industry and labor and all other sections of public opinion, that their feeling is that the idea that 'alcoholism' is an illness 'is true, but not really true.' This feeling will persist until the disease conception of alcoholism attains to clarity and definitiveness."

Despite this grim outlook for an American alcoholism treatment policy rooted in AA's pseudoscientific conception of problem drinking as a disease, Jellinek's book immediately became an instant classic of the alcoholic movement, to this day a misappropriated foundation for treatment policies and programs nationwide. The reason for this is that few people have actually read it from cover to cover, much less contemplated the complicated argument Jellinek put forward. As psychologist and treatment historian William White has observed, "*The Disease Concept of Alcoholism* remains one of the most frequently cited and least read books in the alcoholism field."

Rather, Mann and Smithers and the many AA-minded activists who drove the modern alcoholism movement simply seized on the fact that there now existed a book by a scientist called *The Disease Concept of Alcoholism*, and they held it up as proof of the disease itself. Indeed, the only actual information from the book that has been utilized to any real extent in the alcoholism community since its publication was Jellinek's theory about alpha, beta, gamma, delta, and epsilon alcoholics. This was laid out in a chart that was widely distributed through Mann's vast network of local committees and to the Hazelden-style treatment centers that were popping up across the country, where it was used to convince patients that they were diseased.

Embarrassing Findings

Jellinek's book was more an exercise in semantics than science, because there was still as yet very little scientific study of alcoholism to draw from. In the United States, no federal funds were available for research, and the only philanthropic organization that had taken a major interest in the problem was the one run by R. Brinkley Smithers, who directed its resources toward the NCA and its publicity, research, and lobbying efforts. In England, however, a psychiatrist by the name of D. L. Davies conducted in the early 1960s a long-term follow-up study of ninety-three alcoholic patients at Maudsley Hospital in London, and his report would directly contradict the central component of the conventional disease concept of alcoholism—that true alcoholics can never drink in moderation.

Davies came to the field by happenstance. In his unit at Maudley, Davies always reserved four or five beds for alcoholics, and his staff had a regular procedure of conducting follow-ups after their patients were received. A social worker who worked in Davies's unit reviewed the data from these follow-ups and found that some patients had returned to drinking but without doing damage to their lives. "You realize these people shouldn't happen," the social worker told Davies, to which he replied: "Well they have happened."

Davies launched a deep inquiry, focusing on patients who had been discharged from treatment between seven and eleven years earlier. He found that a significant percentage of them were drinking at levels he described as "normal."

"I wasn't surprised," he would say in a later interview.

> Quite honestly I'd never really given much thought to the outcome of alcoholism. I had never believed that a man could not return to normal drinking. I couldn't see why. I never shared this view. I wasn't very much in the alcoholism field in a way. I was dabbling in it. I had the benefit perhaps of coming with a rather fresh mind to this question, and the outcome didn't seem to me odd at all.

Yet in a paper reporting his findings, which was published in 1962 by the *Quarterly Journal of Studies on Alcohol,* Davies seemed to understand how unusual his findings were. He cautiously framed his findings within commonly held notions about the treatment of alcoholism. "It is not denied that the majority of alcohol addicts are incapable of achieving 'normal drinking,'" he wrote. "All patients should be told to aim at total abstinence."

The *Quarterly Journal of Studies on Alcohol* published eighteen commentaries in response, almost all of which dismissed Davies's findings. They were written by American experts in the fledgling field of alcoholism, nearly all of whom were predisposed to the definition of alcoholism that Mann and the NCA were promoting, the idea that it's a disease that renders its sufferers unable to control their drinking, even after the smallest taste. Davies's findings gravely undermined this notion. So to keep that concept intact, Davies's critics resorted to mental gymnastics.

Among them was Marvin Block, the doctor from Buffalo who had spearheaded the campaign to get the AMA to recognize alcoholism as an illness. Block argued that the study's normal-drinking patients were not alcoholics to begin with, and he noted that the case descriptions for many of them had not noted that they had suffered withdrawal symptoms. Despite the fact that the men had been hospitalized for severe drinking problems, he argued that in his work he'd seen many cases of heavy drinkers whose lives were adversely affected by alcohol abuse but never developed into full-blown alcoholics. It was apparently lost on him that he was describing a dangerous notion that would lead problem drinkers to drink even more—and suffer more consequences—so as to become a textbook example of a sufferer of the disease of alcohol and thereby be ready to embrace the cure.

Block also speculated, without evidence, that these normal-drinking subjects may have undergone a mysterious physical change somewhat like unexpected remissions in cancer patients. "Body chemistry is such that it can change at any time," he wrote. "It is not rare to have spontaneous recoveries from very severe illnesses without the medical profession knowing the cause either of the illness or of its resolution."

Or, he added, as other fellow critics did, that perhaps the reason was that the subjects were Englishmen and as such from a culture with more relaxed attitudes about alcohol, and that in some way led to this outcome.

Though Davies wasn't surprised about the results of his study, he was taken aback by the response to it, which he described in a later interview as an

American reaction, really. I hadn't been to the States at that time and I certainly knew nothing about AA and the alcohol field in the States, and it was only when a friend of mine in the U.S.A. started to write me letters telling me of the outcry that I realized what had happened. I had one letter saying I could never now come to America—the writer said that AA would pelt me with bottles on the airstrip as I arrived.

But not all respondents disputed the results. One, M. L. Seltzer, recalled his own experiences researching controlled drinking, which had produced findings similar to Davies's. He reported reactions similar to the ones Davies was receiving. His findings "prompted the agency that provided funds for the study virtually to order us to omit these 'embarrassing' findings," he wrote. "At a subsequent psychiatric meeting where the paper was presented, a prominent colleague arose to state that the 13 subjects were probably not alcoholics. Similar episodes followed."

Seltzer surmised that the responses were borne less on the spirit of science than on protecting an ideology that was critical for alcoholics—because the "cure" hinged on patients believing that they suffer from a disease that makes it impossible for them to drink like normal people. "Many people working in this field are alcoholics themselves and are compelled to remain abstinent," he wrote. "It may be especially difficult for the alcoholic who must remain dry to accept the idea that others can recover and drink socially. To hear of the 'success' of others may be frustrating—and those workers prefer not to hear about it since it also upsets their treatment concepts."

Insurance for Alcoholics

The controversy over the Davies study unfolded in the pages of an obscure academic journal and had virtually no impact beyond the small community of scientists who were interested in alcoholism and its treatment in the early 1960s. Even among them the report's effects were small, short-lived, and essentially forgotten. On Marty Mann and her nationwide campaign, it had no effect whatsoever. For her purposes, the medical designation of alcoholism as a disease had been firmly established with resolutions passed by the American Medical Association and the World Health Organization in the 1950s—even though neither had in fact called it a disease. She simply misrepresented what both resolutions said so as to support her mission to make treatment of alcoholism a normal and routine part of medical treatment in the United States.

The ultimate goal, of course, was to get problem drinkers into AA—a decidedly nonmedical form of treatment—but the hospitals, clinics, doctors, and nurses could all play a role by stabilizing them with tranquilizers and vitamins and providing a point of contact where they could receive the AA message. Moreover, by enlisting the medical community as first responders in the battle against alcoholism, Mann and her army of volunteers would legitimize the notion that alcoholism is a disease over which the alcoholic is powerless. This was essential, because AA works only if the alcoholic fully accepts this concept.

But as the AMA's 1956 less-than-resounding resolution acknowledging alcoholism as a medical issue revealed, doctors and health care providers were skeptical about treating problem drinkers. So Mann's NCA focused its efforts on the economic driver of America's health care system: industry. In addition to its prodigious public relations campaigns and its lobbying of policy makers at municipal, state, and federal levels, the council devoted much of its energy toward convincing corporate and labor leaders that it would be more profitable to offer treatment and care for the alcoholics in the workforce than to fire them.

Although the NCA's annual conferences were well represented by business and union leaders, the biggest breakthrough in these efforts came from outside the council, on the initiative of an insurance executive who had gotten sober through AA.

James S. Kemper Jr., head of Kemper Insurance, began drinking when he was a freshman at Yale in the 1930s. "I liked how it made me feel," he would later recall in an interview with the *Chicago Tribune*. "Gradually over the years I drank more and more."

In the 1950s, around the time he turned forty, he suffered "a series of disastrous experiences that affected my domestic life, my finances, my friendships and my career." At the time, he was living in Los Angeles, practicing law, and he made his way to an AA meeting. In 1959, with a few years of sobriety under his belt, he took a job at the insurance company his father had founded in 1919, and he quickly rose in the management ranks until he was elected president in 1961.

One of the first things he did in his new role was to establish a program within the company to offer treatment to employees who were having drinking problems. His move was inspired in large part by his own desire to stay sober. "I kept hearing from other recovering alcoholics that helping other people was one good way to stay sober myself," he said. "That was my prime motivation. But, close behind that, I got really interested in the subject of alcoholism as an illness, that it was stigmatic and that the stigma kept many people who could be recovering from seeking help. Here was a frontier in public health, this was 30 years ago, that was nearly unexplored. That fired up my engines."

He was also driven by profits. "The most expensive way to handle alcoholics is to fire or ignore them," he would later explain. "The most profitable and effective way is to help them recover. . . . You also have to consider the cost of bad decisions at upper-management levels, made by alcoholics before you've identified them as such. These savings—from avoiding judgment mistakes in what are multi-million dollar actions in sales, marketing and pricing—are enormous."

Calculating these costs and benefits, Kemper saw that the program paid for itself and then some: "We got that back at least 10 times, perhaps 20 times, in our savings in health insurance, lower absenteeism and employee turnover."

Buoyed by their own success, Kemper began offering coverage of alcoholism to its corporate customers, and soon Kemper's counterparts in the insurance industry began to take notice. "The response of the rest of the industry was skepticism, particularly when we added alcoholism treatment coverage at no extra cost to our policy holders," he told the *Tribune*.

> But two things happened. First, Prudential and a number of other insurance companies followed our lead in offering this benefit. Second, we showed we could offer this benefit and stay competitive. It took the industry a while to recognize that it was already paying for the consequences of alcoholism and to recognize that what we were proposing was to reduce those costs by treating the disease itself.

Companies following Kemper's lead included Blue Cross, Wausau, and Hartford Insurance Group, and throughout the '60s and '70s more would follow suit until by the '80s virtually all insurance companies would offer such coverage, fueling a massive growth in treatment programs that some would come to refer to as "the treatment industrial complex."

Cult or Cure

For its first thirty years of existence, AA had enjoyed nonstop good press, thanks in no small part to Mann's campaign and her genius for PR. But AA received its first major criticism in February 1963, when *Harper's* published "Alcoholics Anonymous: Cult or Cure?" by Arthur H. Cain, a New York psychologist who specialized in helping alcoholics. AA, he wrote, "is becoming one of America's most fanatical religious cults." His barb struck deep because he had worked with AA almost from the beginning and had even been affiliated with Mann's council. But he'd grown troubled by what he saw as a rising wave of fundamentalism in the fellowship.

Claiming he had "no personal axe to grind," he recounted his experiences as a practicing psychologist who specialized in alcohol problems for more than fifteen years in both therapy and research and who had worked closely with Alcoholics Anonymous, the National Council on Alcoholism, and the Christopher D. Smithers Foundation. The overwhelming message he gathered from the meetings he attended was that the Twelve Steps were the only means to recovery; that doctors and psychiatrists simply don't understand alcoholics in the way other alcoholics do; and that these professionals are not only incapable of helping, they're likely to make matters worse. Cain was particularly alarmed by a belief, widely shared in AA meetings, that those alcoholics who couldn't get sober in AA were either not alcoholic to begin with or were helplessly insane. "Frequently in my practice," he wrote, "disillusioned men and women appeal to me: 'Doctor, I've tried AA over and over and I still can't stay sober. There must be something dreadfully wrong with me! What is it?'"

Cain also directed sharp words at the medical community, whom he accused of abdicating their responsibility in treating alcoholics by shunting their patients off to AA meetings, even in cases where the meetings were of no help. As such, he warned that members of AA were quietly—anonymously—changing policy regarding alcohol in the country.

> AAs hold key positions in city, state, and private agencies dealing with alcoholism. Many executive directors of local committees and information centers are members of AA. This means that public education on alcoholism is almost entirely in the hands of AAs. Furthermore, nearly all information about research, treatment, and community action is disseminated by public-relations directors who adhere to the AA party line. Thus, almost everything we read on alcoholism in newspapers and magazines is AA propaganda.

"One result of this authoritarianism," he continued, "is that well-meaning laymen organize committees and sponsor 'research'—which leads qualified professionals to assume that the job of fighting alcoholism is getting done. But it isn't."

Cain wrote another article published a little more than a year later, in September 1964, in the *Saturday Evening Post*, titled "Alcoholics Can Be Cured—Despite AA." In this piece, he ratcheted up his criticism, claiming,

> AA has become a dogmatic cult whose chapters too often turn sobriety into slavery to AA. Because of its narrow outlook, Alcoholics Anonymous prevents thousands from ever being cured. Moreover AA has retarded scientific research into one of America's most serious health

problems. With this growing dogmatism came a Dark Ages attitude
toward any scientist who might differ with official AA doctrine.

This dogma, he wrote, impeded scientific investigations and prevented doctors and therapists from treating patients in ways that contradicted the AA
prescription. He offered the example of a New York City hospital where the
physicians preferred using paraldehyde, which is a form of alcohol, to treat acute
intoxication. But then members of AA threatened to stop referring patients
there if they didn't stop using the drug. Bending to the pressure, the hospital
switched to chloral hydrate, which is alcohol-free but a more toxic drug.

Cain expanded the argument he'd made in the *Harper's* piece that Mann's
group, the NCA, acted as a "propaganda unit" for AA and was infecting public
policy discourse about the problem of excessive drinking. "I once heard Arthur
Flemming, former Secretary of Health, Education and Welfare, read verbatim a
pronouncement on alcoholism which I knew had been prepared a year earlier by
NCA's public-relations firm," he wrote, referring to an instance where Flemming
repeated a figure based on the study Bunky Jellinek had done at Yale at Marty
Mann's request, the one that he himself had warned in the report itself was flawed.

AA members felt attacked. After the issue of the *Saturday Evening Post* hit
stands, the NCA issued a memorandum to all of its local affiliates with direction about how to respond to the article. "The policy of the National office will
be to give an INDIRECT answer, NOT a direct rebuttal to the recent article by
Arthur Cain in the Post. The mis-statements in the article are so gross that a
whole history of the alcoholism movement would have to be written to establish in the minds of the casual reader the difference between fact and fancy."

But AA's cofounder Bill Wilson was circumspect. In his column in the
Grapevine, under the title "Our Critics Can Be Our Benefactors," he offered
readers excerpts of pieces he had written in the past about being open to new
ideas and offered a few excerpts. One read:

> It would be a product of false pride to believe that Alcoholics Anony-
> mous is a cure-all, even for alcoholism. Here we must remember
> our debt to the men of medicine. Here we must be friendly and,
> above all, open minded toward every new development in the medical
> or psychological art that promises to be helpful to sick people. We
> should always be friendly to those in the fields of alcoholic research,

rehabilitation, and education. . . . Let us constantly remind ourselves that the experts in religion are the clergymen; that the practice of medicine is for physicians; and that we, the recovered alcoholics, are their assistants.

In other words, he was basically affirming that Cain was right, and he concluded his collection of excerpts from earlier writings by preaching that "just as each member of AA must continue to take his moral inventory and act upon it, so must our whole Society do if we are to survive and if we are to serve usefully and well."

This seems surprising coming from the cofounder of AA, but in his own life and activities, Wilson himself had at the time of these articles' release sought to expand notions of recovery beyond that defined and promulgated by AA. In 1955, he had formally stepped away from the organization as its titular leader, though he remained active, working at AA's headquarters one or two days a week and writing articles for the *Grapevine*. This move came in part as a result of his own unsuccessful efforts to transform AA into something more than "the spiritual kindergarten" he'd come up with in his early sobriety, when he wrote the Big Book and the Twelve Steps. He tried to revise both, to make them more comprehensive and mature, but his fellow alcoholics fought him. "As to changing the Steps themselves, or even the text of the AA book," Wilson would later say, "I am assured by many that I could certainly be excommunicated if a word were touched. It is a strange fact of human nature that when a spiritually centered movement starts and finally adopts certain principles, these finally freeze absolutely solid."

When Wilson wrote the Big Book, he filled it with promises that would be delivered to anyone who worked the AA program with honesty and diligence. But by any honest assessment these promises didn't come true for him. A prolific adulterer who couldn't seem to stop his sexual trysts, he suffered from guilt that plunged him into long periods of debilitating depression. He sought help from places other than AA and began seeing a psychologist and working with a Catholic priest, Father Ed Dowling. For a while Wilson considered converting to Catholicism, though this too sparked controversy in AA, so he set the idea aside. He dove into spiritualism; he and Lois set up a "spook room" where they'd hold séances and lay their hands on a Ouija board, and he believed spirits were guiding him, in particular a fifteenth-century monk named Boniface.

He began looking for remedies beyond the Twelve Steps, for himself and for alcoholics who couldn't find sobriety in the program. To this end, he experimented with LSD, taking the drug while it was still legal, under the supervision of a psychologist and with Aldous Huxley and Gerald Heard (he also shared it with his wife and other members of AA, possibly including Marty Mann, who over the years had explored Zen Buddhism, tai chi, and transcendental meditation, which she particularly loved). He hoped it might evoke in alcoholics the kind of spiritual experience he'd had in detox, under the influence of belladonna. His fellow members of AA were appalled by the notion, and they prevailed on him to shut up about it. Same thing with his growing interest in niacin, or vitamin B3, as a mood stabilizer for alcoholics with depression. He wrote to members of AA and to doctors, on AA stationery, urging them to try it—rankling AA members who implored him to not associate AA's name with this or any other alternative form of treatment.

Rising Power

Time would reveal how prescient Cain's critique was; it was virtually identical to criticisms of AA that are still raised today. When it came out, though, it did little more than galvanize AA dogma, and it was buried under the continuing onslaught of positive press for the twelve-step approach. Mann's media machine simply kept rolling on.

At the NCA's annual meeting in 1963, R. Brinkley Smithers, then the council's president, bragged about changing public opinion about alcoholics and alcoholism. "In the area of motion pictures, there is the widely acclaimed *Days of Wine and Roses*. In television, many of you will remember stories about alcoholism that appeared on *Armstrong Circle Theatre*, *Alfred Hitchcock Presents*, *Ben Casey*, *Doctor Kildare*, and David Susskind's *Open End*." He cited a series of Associated Press articles, as well as articles in *Good Housekeeping*, *This Week*, and a glowing profile of Marty Mann in *Reader's Digest*.

Though Mann was already well known from her many radio and TV appearances, this latter piece really brought her to life for readers around the world. "She is anything but a hatchet-bearing Carrie Nation," the author wrote. "She has no quarrel with the drinker who can drink safely and socially. But when she faces ignorance and prejudice about alcoholism, she becomes a 'seized' woman, an intense and relentless crusader. 'Lovely, but with a sword'—they say of her."

The story includes a hilarious anecdote:

> One day on a Fifth Avenue bus, a much martini-ed up business man sat down beside her, and started a conversation. Marty knew an alcoholic when she saw one. And she knew the peculiar penetrating odor that comes from the pores when he is far gone. Sympathetic, but ever crusading, she let him talk.
>
> "How about dinner, honey?" he proposed before her street came up.
> "Sure!"
> "Where?"
> "I'll meet you at 133 East 39th Street at 8:15."
> The address was that of Alcoholics Anonymous. The drunk, fortified by further martinis in the interim, was there. And, amused by Marty's ingenuity, he stayed. A new vista opened up for him.

The article was years in the making, due to Mann's wrangling over the content. Her archives contain a thick file of correspondence about the piece, with multiple drafts marked up by Mann. Her primary concern was that the magazine not disclose her membership in AA, and these records reveal just how diligently she protected her own image and that of AA.

"I strenuously object to the word 'degradation,'" referring to an early draft's description of her hard-drinking days, "which did not occur in my case, at least not in the sense in which it is usually used, and in which it would be understood by the reader. I suggest substituting the word 'defeat,' or the word 'despair.'" And, she added, "I deeply dislike the phrase 'falling-down drunk.' Especially since I *didn't* fall down. How about 'very drunk' or 'really drunk'? Nor, incidentally, did I ever 'sell my possessions for whiskey.'"

But while positive press coverage was Mann's wheelhouse, her ultimate aim was to affect public policy. During the mid-1960s, she spoke to numerous state legislatures, including those of Tennessee and South Carolina (the first woman ever to have done so). From the Nebraska legislature she received honorary induction into the Great Navy of the State of Nebraska, declaring her "a good fellow and loyal friend and counselor."

Over the years Mann's campaign made steady progress toward its holy grail: a national system for identifying and treating alcoholism based on AA. At the NCA's 1964 annual meeting, Mann said,

Another major event has been the entrance of the Federal Government in a really big way into the field of alcoholism. This is something for which we at the National Council have been working for 15 years. I spearheaded much of that work because I'm the peripatetic one and I get around, and I've been back and forth to Washington talking to this one and that one both publicly and privately.

They started making inroads during the administration of President Dwight Eisenhower. Ike's director of the National Institute of Mental Health appeared at several NCA annual conferences and delivered speeches about alcoholism as a health problem (though, to Mann's great annoyance, he would sometimes refer to alcoholism as "the Irishman's disease" and pepper his speeches with references to "skid row drunks"). So favorable was the Republican administration to the cause that Mann was pulling heavily for Richard Nixon to win. As it turned out, John F. Kennedy was a better champion for Mann's cause, because he made mental health a centerpiece of his domestic health policy, whereas Nixon was notoriously averse to psychology. The Kennedy administration awarded the first federal grant to address the issue of alcoholism, devoting $1.1 million to fund a newly formed Cooperative Commission on the Study of Alcoholism, launched in 1961. The commission would take six years to issue its report, much of which would be at odds with Mann's message, but its very creation added to the momentum of Mann's mission: the federal government was taking seriously the notion that problem drinking is a public health issue.

There was movement in the legislative branch as well. Beginning in 1962 and every year during the 1960s, US Representative Elliot Hagan of Georgia introduced a bill that would establish a federal commission on alcoholism, a fully funded program of research on alcoholism, public information, and treatment programs. He'd been a champion of rehabilitation programs for alcoholics since before he'd gotten into politics, inspired to take action after seeing a close friend succumb to heavy drinking. As a Georgia state representative prior to ascending to Washington, he had introduced and passed similar bills there and had also founded a rehab center in his home state that offered an array of medical and psychological strategies to address the problem. Along with the Yale clinics, it was seen as a potential model to be replicated across the United States before being beat out by the Minnesota Model.

That same year, Anthony Celebrezze was appointed secretary of health, education, and welfare, and he strongly advocated for the cause of alcoholism. In July 1963 he convened a National Conference on Alcoholism, after which he formed a Committee on Alcoholism, to which he appointed Mann. Two other members of the committee had worked with one of her local groups in Michigan, so her campaign had now gained a toehold in the White House. After Kennedy was assassinated in November of that year, a card-carrying member of her organization moved into the Oval Office.

Presidential Seal of Approval

From the time he was sworn in as president and through his landslide election in 1964, Lyndon Johnson kept the issue of alcoholism alive in his ambitious Great Society domestic agenda, monitoring the progress of the National Conference on Alcoholism established under the Kennedy administration and sending letters and proclamations of support to Mann and the NCA for each of their annual conferences. "For more than two decades you have provided pioneering leadership in seeking knowledge, treatment, and prevention of an affliction which has long caused a tragic waste of mankind," Johnson wrote on the occasion of the NCA's 1965 annual gathering. "Your meeting this year coincides with a new national determination to bring alcoholism under control. Only through a dedicated partnership of effort—voluntary, private, and public—can we succeed in achieving this goal."

Then, on March 1, 1966, the president revealed what his administration had in mind. In a Special Message to the Congress on Domestic Health and Education, he threw the full force of the White House bully pulpit behind the cause.

"The alcoholic suffers from a disease which will yield eventually to scientific research and adequate treatment," he declared to the nation's lawmakers. "Even with the present limited state of our knowledge, much can be done to reduce the untold suffering and uncounted waste caused by this affliction."

He laid out a plan of action to address it, stating that he had "instructed the Secretary of Health, Education, and Welfare to":

- "appoint an Advisory Committee on Alcoholism"
- "establish in the Public Health Service a center for research on the cause, prevention, control and treatment of alcoholism"

- "develop an education program in order to foster public understanding based on scientific fact"
- "work with public and private agencies on the state and local level to include this disease in comprehensive health programs"

(Marked-up copies of early drafts in Johnson's archives reveal that there had been a fifth directive—"encourage recognition of alcoholism as a disease by the health insurance issue"—but one of the president's top aides, Joseph Califano Jr., wrote in the margins in red pencil: "Are we taking too big of a bite here? 5 million alcoholics can raise the rates." And the provision was cut.)

By then, thirty-seven states had passed laws referring to alcoholism as an illness or disease, but Johnson was the first president ever to have publicly used the terminology. Johnson's archives reveal that some on the White House staff had misgivings about the declaration. Colin M. MacLeod, deputy director of the White House Office of Science and Technology, wrote in a letter in response to a call for comment on the speech: "The view that alcoholism is *a* single disease is an oversimplification. We know that it is a symptom of some diseases, as well as a response to frustration." But there's no evidence in the files at Johnson's presidential library in Austin that MacLeod's concerns were given serious consideration.

Ecstatic, Mann immediately responded with a handwritten letter to the president. "It is my prayerful hope that, despite the thousands of letters you receive, you will yourself see this letter, which is most urgently and personally addressed to you in gratitude and appreciation," she wrote.

> In this I speak both for myself as a recovered alcoholic and long-time worker in this field, and also, I deeply believe, I speak for all those millions of alcoholics, recovered and non-recovered, who will benefit—in some cases will have the chance to live—because of what you have said.
>
> The words you spoke in your Health Message to Congress were historic words. No president before you dared brave the stigma, the long neglect, the ridicule and misunderstanding surrounding this vast and devastating problem. Your call to action was to me a daring and splendid act, worthy of your high office and of your own high aims.

She recalled when she'd first met Johnson in 1945 on a trip to Texas to establish one of the NCA's earliest local committees there and again in 1946 and how important it was to their fledgling organization that he, a sitting congressman, would agree to serve on the Austin committee's board of directors. "I knew that one day we would have your support at the national level, when the spade work had been done, and the soil was ready," her letter concluded. "That time has come. And you have spoken."

Douglass Cater, special assistant to the president, wrote in response,

> The President has asked me to thank you for your warm and thoughtful letter of March 9, and for your strong support for his actions to deal with alcoholism as a public health issue. As you know, the President is eager to see the Federal Government deal vigorously with this problem, which touches nearly every American family. As he goes forward with his efforts, he is deeply grateful for the heroic work which you and your colleagues are doing in this field.

Mann was appointed to the committee Johnson had called for, which promptly began discussing legislative action to address alcoholism. At the time of Johnson's speech, there were several alcoholism bills in Congress asking for as much as $46 million for research, and Johnson's own Economic Opportunity Amendments of 1966 sought to devote $10 million to develop treatment programs in communities across the United States. Following the Minnesota Model for treatment, the amendment called for the hiring and training of recovered alcoholics to work as counselors. As the midterm elections approached, the NCA issued a memorandum to its affiliates urging them to ask their congressional candidates where they stand on these bills and on the issue of alcoholism.

In late October of that year, at the height of the midterm election season, John W. Gardner, Johnson's new secretary of health, education, and welfare, called a press conference to announce his responses to the president's mandate. "Four to five million Americans are alcoholics," he told the reporters, "and the burden of their alcoholism is not carried by them alone. It directly—and often tragically—affects between 16 and 20 million members of their families."

He recommended the creation of a National Center for the Prevention and Control of Alcoholism within the National Institute of Mental Health, with the goal of "making the best treatment and rehabilitation services available to those who need them now," pursuing a long-range goal of developing more effective means of prevention and rehabilitation.

Not long after Johnson's historic declaration of alcoholism as a disease, a man named Donald B. Lee wrote a letter to him. He'd been an acquaintance of the president's when they had both served in the US Navy, and he wrote that he'd struggled with alcoholism but was sober thanks to AA. In the process of straightening his life out, he'd become affiliated with a nonprofit in Millerton, New York, called My Brother's Place, a halfway house that provided therapy to alcoholics based on AA, "which itself has provided the most successful treatment known for the disease," though he was quick to add: "I must point out, however, that the program proposed by 'My Brother's Place' is in no way affiliated with AA, but would derive substantial support, service and guidance from scores of persons who achieved sobriety through the AA program."

Lee told Johnson that the program had submitted a grant request to the National Institutes of Health for $611,000 to cover a three-year pilot, and he asked if the president might throw his muscle behind it and free the funds up for their project. Johnson's assistant secretary for health and scientific affairs wrote back, stating that the president had instructed the Department of Health, Education, and Welfare to "institute a national program on alcoholism" and that Lee's "proposed project may fit into the plans now being developed."

Though the administration didn't get behind the program Lee championed, Johnson's call for action would ultimately bring into being a national alcoholism treatment program very much like the one Lee was involved in—not officially connected to AA but in all manners of action, absolutely tied in with AA's mission and continued growth.

Court Approval

At the time Johnson made his statement on alcoholism, drunkenness was a crime in most states, and this as much as anything motivated his administration to tackle the issue, Joseph Califano told me in an interview. "We were conscious of the cost of alcohol abuse, and we viewed it from the viewpoint of the states treating drunkenness as a crime," he said. "With the president's message, we wanted to make the distinction that just being drunk was a health care problem, not a criminal justice problem."

But the Johnson administration's power to do this was limited. The task force Johnson called for could produce volumes of information and from the bully pulpit the president could deliver it to the nation, but the administration couldn't compel individual states to stop treating problem drinking as a crime and begin addressing it as a medical issue. Only the nation's courts could.

Around the time that Johnson made his statement on alcoholism, the leaders of the Washington, DC, local organizing committee of the NCA approached the powerful law firm of Covington & Burling and asked it to challenge the designation of drunkenness as a crime under the same premise of the *Robinson v. California* case, that punishing a drug addict for simply being an addict is a violation of the Eighth Amendment protecting against cruel and unusual punishment. The firm's partners agreed to take up the cause, and they chose a young associate named Peter Barton Hutt to carry it through.

"One day I was walking down the hall when a senior associate pulled me aside and asked, 'Have you done anything useful lately?'" Hutt recalled to me in an interview.

"'Well, no,' he replied. 'What do you have in mind?'"

Hutt began visiting the city's drunk tank in the evenings and the wee morning hours. The place was filthy and it reeked, he recalled, but there was no shortage of potential clients. The problem was that every time he signed on as the attorney for one of them, the district attorney, Milton Korman, would drop the case. Korman had a reputation for holding a dim view of drunks, believing they were beyond hope for rehabilitation, and he prosecuted them routinely and mercilessly. But when he faced a worthy opponent in Hutt and his firm, he backed off. So Hutt took a highly unusual position for a defense attorney—he asked the judge to reject Korman's dismissal of the charges and demand that he prosecute. "It was hilarious that the defense attorney was arguing in court in favor of prosecution," Hutt said, "and the prosecutor was arguing against prosecution."

Hutt finally got his day in court in September 1964, defending a man named DeWitt Easter. Sixty years old, a plasterer by trade, Easter had been a heavy drinker since the 1930s. He'd been convicted of public intoxication about seventy times. The ACLU helped Hutt on the case, and they argued that Easter suffered from chronic alcoholism. In municipal court, the high-powered team of lawyers put all their might behind the case, calling in doctors and experts to testify that Easter had lost control over his drinking because he suffered from a disease of the mind and body that made him powerless over alcohol. In his closing arguments, Hutt likened Easter to an epileptic who had had a seizure in public and was subsequently arrested for disorderly conduct. The Eighth Amendment of the Constitution prohibiting cruel and unusual punishment would preclude such punishment, Hutt argued.

The judge wasn't convinced, and he rendered the verdict Hutt and his team were hoping for: guilty. They appealed, and, true to plan, the conviction was upheld. In this instance, however, the judges' decision showed Hutt's argument was gaining traction. The judges agreed that Easter suffered from the disease that made him unable to control his drinking, but he was arrested for being drunk in public, not simply for being drunk or being an alcoholic; if he'd been drunk in private, it wouldn't have been a crime.

Hutt took Easter's case to a federal court, and the eight judges unanimously agreed that the conviction should be reversed. It was a momentary victory for Easter (who would never recover from his alcoholism and ultimately burn to death after passing out with a lit cigarette), but not for Hutt and company. Their goal had been to take the case to the Supreme Court, where the question of whether alcoholism should be a crime would be settled for the entire nation.

Time magazine ran an article about Easter's case, and attorneys for another alcoholic in North Carolina read it. They contacted Hutt. In this case, a man named Driver had been convicted of public intoxication in Durham and sentenced to two years. His record included two hundred such arrests and convictions. Hutt signed on, and again they won in a federal court, this time a southern one, which was quite an accomplishment. "Other than in the Civil Rights field," Hutt said, "I can think of no case in the past 20 years in which a southern U.S. court of appeals struck down a state statute on grounds of unconstitutionality."

In their decision, the judges wrote: "This addiction—chronic alcoholism— is now almost universally accepted as a disease. The symptoms . . . may appear as 'disorder of behavior.' Obviously, this includes appearances in public, as here, unwilled and ungovernable by the victim. When that is the conduct for which he is criminally accused, there can be no judgment of conviction passed upon him."

It was another victory for Hutt, but for his purposes, a loss. He'd have to wait a couple more years before the nation's highest court would weigh in on the question of alcoholism as a disease.

Science Strikes Back, and Misses

While alcoholism cases were making their way up the court system and alcoholism bills were being considered on Capitol Hill, the federally funded initiative to combat alcoholism languished. The Cooperative Commission on the Study of Alcoholism, founded in 1961 with a $1.1 million grant from the National Institute of Mental Health, housed at Stanford, had been at work for several years and was nearing the end of its five-year period with almost nothing to show for it.

The initiative had arisen out of talks between scientists and doctors who had assumed leadership roles at various newly formed state agencies concerned with alcoholism. These agencies had been formed largely in response to the lobbying of Mann's organization, but nearly all of the professionals behind the Cooperative Commission were from outside of AA and part of their motivation for the initiative grew out of a desire to circumvent AA's and Mann's influence.

Bunky Jellinek returned from Europe to serve on the commission, but he died soon after, leaving the initiative without its most experienced and enthusiastic member. R. Nevitt Sanford, then a professor of psychology and education at Stanford, had been chosen to lead the commission, but he had no background in alcoholism research and, as it turned out, no interest in it either. He used the NIMH grant money to pay for fellowships at a research organization he was establishing at Stanford called the Institute for the Study of Human Problems. So as the commission neared its deadline, its members scrambled to host a series of conferences for the purposes of preparing a policy paper that could be presented to the public.

The subsequent report flatly rejected the term alcoholism, opting instead for "problem drinking," because alcoholism, the authors believed, was too limiting a term; it didn't encompass the full range of problems associated with alcohol. They warned that using "alcoholism" to describe all aspects of problem drinking "is not desirable" because it might lead to "stereotyping and a gross oversimplification." They zeroed in on the disease concept. They singled out the issue of "motivation" as particularly problematic.

> It is often assumed motivation is an all-or-none phenomenon: otherwise, nothing is done until the patient decides he wants to stop drinking—as though the motivated patient were worthy of assistance and

the non-motivated one not. (The same concern about a patient's "readiness" is found in Alcoholics Anonymous groups, where reference is made to persons not yet having "reached bottom.")

The report criticized AA's rejection of public health as part of the treatment model and doctors for shirking their responsibility by simply referring alcoholics to AA. "The clearly stated rules and principles of A.A. have been a help to many problem drinkers, although serving as a barrier for some others."

The commission argued that AA had come into conflict with professional agencies. "Many in AA feel strongly that there is no need for other services and programs except for medical management of the toxic effects of alcohol in the rehabilitation of problem drinkers," the report stated. "On the other hand, some segments of the public and some community caregivers expect AA to assume the major role in the rehabilitation of these persons. The existence of AA is even used to sometimes justify the absence of professionally directed services."

Its main recommendations were to:

- Establish a national center on alcoholism to drive national policy
- Begin a national research program on alcoholism and a national program of alcohol education
- Designate state and local agencies for alcoholism treatment and prevention efforts
- Decriminalize alcoholism
- Develop a network of local treatment centers
- Train health service workers on how to deal with alcoholics
- Make alcoholism treatment an insurance benefit
- Develop a variety of treatment approaches

Most daringly, it stressed ways by which America might normalize drinking so as to prevent abuse. For example, the commission suggested teaching kids about alcohol in school and allowing liquor advertisements to show whole families, kids and all, drinking. It urged colleges to serve beer in their cafeterias and churches to give wine to children at their events. The commission based these on looking at other cultures, such as France and Italy, where alcohol use was seen as not so much of a big deal and drinking is associated with other activities.

The commission members had expected the NIMH to endorse the report and make it known to the public. But the agency thought it too controversial because of the suggestions to normalize drinking, and it backed away from its own million-dollar project. The commission turned to the National Council of Churches, which agreed to officially receive the report and make recommendations to its members based on its findings. The report got publicity but not the kind the commission had hoped for—headlines that read, Teach Young People to Drink, Panel Urges and More Family Drinking to Reduce Alcoholism.

Angry letters came pouring in from Christians across the country who were alarmed by this apparent call for more drinking, and the National Council of Churches immediately sought to distance itself from the controversial report. In news stories, journalists ignored the criticism of the concept of alcoholism Mann was peddling, its argument that it "can readily lead to oversimplification and stereotyping of problem drinkers." They also overlooked the criticism of AA, the way its members discouraged doctors, psychologists, psychiatrists, and social workers from becoming involved in the treatment process, believing instead that the best remedy is a drunk working with another drunk.

Mann and the NCA likewise cherry-picked from the commission's findings and recommendations. They heralded the report's recommendations on the decriminalization of public drunkenness, that insurers provide for alcoholism treatment and, above all, the creation of a federal agency on alcoholism. Everything else they ignored, and so did the reporters on the story. Anything that didn't fit the Marty Mann storyline got zero attention.

Split Decision in the Highest Court

With LBJ in the White House and numerous alcoholism bills rising through Congress, Mann's dream of a national program for alcoholism treatment was on the very brink of coming true. At the same time, though, the unrelenting war in Vietnam threatened to bring it down along with its powerful champion, whose popularity had soared just a few years earlier but was now plummeting. Desperate to keep Johnson in power and to keep the alcoholism initiative alive, Mann sent the president a telegram on March 13, 1968:

STAND FAST MR PRESIDENT THE PEOPLE ARE BEHIND YOU REGARD-
LESS OF VERY QUESTIONABLE POLLS I TRAVEL CONSTANTLY AND MY
READINGS SHOW THE PEOPLE KNOW YOU ARE A GREAT LEADER AND
A GREAT AMERICAN KNOWING OF YOUR COURAGE AND HUMANITY IN
SUPPORTING THE UNPOPULAR CAUSE OF ALCOHOLISM IN THE EARLY
DAYS OF THE FORTIES IN AUSTIN TEXAS ADDS MY DEEP RESPECT
FOR YOUR STEADFASTNESS.

On the same day she mailed Johnson a formal letter "to offer you my services if you feel they could be of assistance," writing that "in my humble opinion the Administration needs a powerful and constant Public Information program, preferably carried by the people directly to the people and giving them the unbiased information the press in my opinion does not supply."

She gave her PR credentials, boasted of her ability to speak "powerfully and dynamically," adding "I have such deep and abiding convictions about you as a great President, a great leader, and a great American. I stand wholeheartedly with you in your leadership on Vietnam and on our social problems."

In the margins of her letter, an aide called for staff to send a "Note from White House. Thanks for telegram, appreciate support." Sadly for Mann, two weeks later, Johnson delivered his "I will not seek, and I shall not accept, the nomination of my party for another term as your president" speech to the nation.

The same week that Mann sent her letter, the Supreme Court heard oral arguments in the case of a man named Leroy Powell, who had been arrested in Austin in 1966 for stumbling down the street, drunk. He earned his living shining shoes in a local bar, and he'd been arrested more than a hundred times before. Busted again, he was found guilty in court and fined $20. Being broke, he had to work off the fine by doing menial labor in the jail for $5 a day.

His defense attorney reached out to Peter Hutt, the young attorney from Covington & Burling who had won victories for the disease concept of alcohol in federal appeals courts. He agreed to help take Powell's case all the way to the Supreme Court. He prepared a court brief that was endorsed by the ACLU, AMA, and an array of church, law enforcement, and alcoholism groups, but Mann's organization refused to sign on because of Powell's indigence; her campaign had been to remove the stigma associated with alcoholism, to move the public mind away from the idea of an alcoholic as a derelict drunk. The Powell case, Mann argued, might damage the image of the alcoholic.

As he got ready to appear before the justices, Hutt read Jellinek's book, *The Disease Concept of Alcoholism*, which was often referred to in arguments supporting the medical approach to the problem. As he read he was stunned to find that the book in fact raised serious questions about the notion that alcoholism is a disease and provided little evidence to substantiate the claim. "I got through it and realized there's nothing to it," he told me in an interview. "It didn't give me anything to argue with." He described it as a "mishmash."

Nonetheless, he believed his argument went over well, and he'd heard from Supreme Court clerks that the decision would be in his favor. But then he learned that Chief Justice Earl Warren, who was opposed to the appeal, had persuaded Justice Thurgood Marshall to his side, offering Marshall the opportunity to write the majority opinion.

The final decision lacked a full majority, however; it was 4–4–1, with three justices—Marshall, Hugo Black, and John Marshall Harlan—supporting Marshall's finding that "there is no agreement among medical experts as to what it means to say that 'alcoholism' is a 'disease,' or upon the 'manifestations of alcoholism,' or the nature of a 'compulsion'" and that Powell's conviction should be upheld.

Concluding that Powell should be exonerated on the grounds of his medical condition were William O. Douglas, William J. Brennan, Potter Stewart, and Abe Fortas, who wrote:

> Although many aspects of the disease remain obscure, there are some hard facts—medical and, especially, legal facts—that are accessible to us and that provide a context in which the case may be analyzed. We are similarly woefully deficient in our medical, diagnostic, and therapeutic knowledge of mental disease and the problem of insanity; but few would urge that, because of this, we should totally reject the legal significance of what we do know about these phenomena.

And alone in the middle was Byron White. Referring to an earlier Supreme Court case, *Robinson v. California*, in which it was deemed a violation of the Eighth Amendment to punish a drug addict simply for being an addict, he asserted that while this precedent would support the view that a chronic alcoholic with an irresistible urge to consume alcohol should not be punishable for drinking or being drunk, appellant's conviction was for the different crime of being drunk in a public place, and though appellant showed that he was to some degree compelled to drink and that he was drunk at the time of his arrest, [Powell] made no showing that he was unable to stay off the streets at that time.

In other words, Powell wasn't arrested for being drunk; he was arrested for being drunk in public, which he had the wherewithal to avoid.

It's a fascinating decision, one referred to in many other cases and taught perennially in criminal law classes. Hutt counts it as a win and a loss. While a slim majority of justices agreed to uphold Powell's conviction, the same narrow margin of votes—one—affirmed that alcoholism is a disease. Despite this, critics of the disease concept of alcoholism point to the case as strong evidence of their own cause.

In his majority opinion, Marshall quotes a long exchange from the transcript of Powell's trial in county court. During cross-examination, the state's attorney asked him if he'd had a drink that morning.

"Yes, sir," Powell said.

"And you knew that, if you drank it, you could keep on drinking and get drunk?"

"Well, I was supposed to be here on trial, and I didn't take but that one drink."

"So you exercised your willpower and kept from drinking anything today but that one drink?"

"Yes, sir, that's right."

But on redirect, his own lawyer asked, "Leroy, isn't the real reason why you had just one drink today because you just had enough money to buy one drink? . . . That's what really controlled the amount you drank this morning, isn't it?"

"Yes, sir."

Law of the Land

As the 1960s came to an end and Johnson retired to his ranch and turned the White House over to Nixon, Marty Mann had good reason for concern. Despite her support of Nixon in 1960, the incoming president had revealed by the end of the decade that he was no champion of LBJ's Great Society initiatives. What's more, he was notoriously averse to psychological programs, in no small part because the Kennedys had championed them and he loathed the Kennedys. A national policy and program on alcoholism was not a priority for him.

But she would soon learn that it wouldn't matter who was in the White House. The ultimate champion of her cause would be sworn in on the other side of the National Mall—a freshman senator from Iowa named Harold Hughes.

Hughes's biography was a fulsome embodiment of the AA story of alcoholism as a disease. A truck driver in his early career, he had his first taste of alcohol in his teens and immediately took to it. "When I took a drink I never wanted to stop," he would write in his autobiography, *The Man from Ida Grove.* "Some sort of a chemical process took place in my body making me want to drink three for every one someone else drank."

He went on a prodigious bender, at the end of which his wife filed a request for him to be committed to an asylum, which he got a lawyer to beat, on the promise he quit for a year. He quit for a while, then he told himself "Just one drink" and went to a bar, coming home hours later, smashed. For weeks and months he drank, and the more he did, the lower his spirits sank, until finally, in the depths of despair, he grabbed a shotgun and hunkered down in a bathtub to shoot himself in the head.

But in a moment of hesitation he prayed, "Whatever You ask me to do, Father, I will do it." Then he put down the shotgun and opened a Bible and prayed some more.

Newly saved, he started an AA group in his hometown, Ida Grove. With his head clear, he became interested in politics. He rose in the ranks of his union, was appointed to the Iowa Better Trucking Bureau, and was eventually elected to the Iowa State Commerce Commission. In 1960 he ran for governor and lost, but two years later he ran again and won. The first meeting he held in the governor's office was an AA meeting, with his home group.

During his first term, he established a state-run treatment program for alcoholics that followed the AA-based Minnesota Model, and he led the repeal of the state's dry laws, allowing purchase of liquor by the drink. His own Methodist church ran a coordinated campaign against the law. "I was fighting my old enemy in a new way," he would later write. The law was easy to thwart.

All across the state were "clubs" where drinkers could pay a membership fee and drink from a bottle they brought, paying for the ice and glass. Some clubs would illegally sell bottles at inflated prices. Because they operated outside the law, no one checked IDs, so minors could be served.

Early on during his time in the governor's office, he positioned himself as an ally of President Johnson, spending the night at the White House and winning lots of federal funds to establish more treatment facilities in Iowa. But as the Vietnam War grew more and more intractable, he came out against it. On a peace platform, he ran for the US Senate in 1968 and not only won but built for himself a national reputation, arriving in Washington amid speculation that he might soon wind up in the White House.

His status as a recovering alcoholic was known by then. During his bid for reelection as governor in 1964, *Look* magazine ran a profile that outed him. His opponent tried to make an issue of it, but it backfired and made Hughes more likable. He was seen as a man of strong faith, and when he got to the Senate, he strengthened this impression by claiming an empty office and turning it into a prayer and meditation room. He'd later joke that hard-drinking members of both chambers of Congress would duck and hide when they saw him coming.

New to Capitol Hill, he was looking for a project to latch onto. He saw that the Department of Health, Education, and Welfare allocated only $4 million in community grants for alcoholism treatment programs and wondered "how could we reconcile this puny effort with spending $25 million for one bomber, many of which were now being downed in Vietnam?" He learned that several other senators had been trying for years to get the Senate to consider alcohol legislation. To move these ideas forward, he asked the chair of the Labor and Public Welfare Committee to let him establish a special subcommittee on alcoholism and drug addiction.

The chair of the committee, Ralph Yarborough, a Democrat from Texas, said Hughes could have his subcommittee but no funds to operate it. "I'll do it with volunteers," Hughes replied, undaunted. "They're all over the place. They're everywhere. I can get people to run the subcommittee and it won't cost you a dime."

True to his prediction, hundreds of recovering alcoholics reached out to work for him, volunteering their time. "Many of these were dedicated people who later played an important role in developing the alcoholism legislation he sponsored," his top legislative aide, Nancy Olson, later wrote in a book about Hughes's efforts.

Hughes took speaking engagements and donated his honorariums to the cause, an amount he later estimated at about $15,000.

Out of this self-funded, AA-driven initiative came the proposed Comprehensive Alcohol Abuse and Alcoholism Prevention, Treatment, and Rehabilitation Act, or Hughes Act, which would provide federal funding and support for community-based treatment programs, for public information campaigns to prevent alcohol abuse, and for scientific research. To carry out these initiatives, it would create a new division in the National Institutes of Health devoted entirely to alcohol problems.

The first hearings for the bill were held in early 1969 and were televised on national TV. The crowds were standing room only. Marty Mann was the first witness, and she testified as head of the NCA, not a member of AA. During her testimony, Mann called the bill "an emancipation proclamation for alcoholics." She identified herself as a recovering alcoholic but didn't disclose the fact that her sobriety had come through AA, nor did any of the other many AA members who testified on the bill's behalf. "AA, because of its traditions, does not as an organization take a position on outside issues, but individual members were a major force in influencing our work," Olson later explained.

The only AA member to disclose his affiliation was AA's cofounder, Bill Wilson, though Hughes ordered the news cameramen in attendance to not show his face, and they complied. Wilson called the bill the "Big Twelfth Step Effort"—a reference to the step that calls on members to share the message of AA and said "for me this is an extremely moving and significant occasion. This is splashdown day for the Apollo."

He limited himself to talking about AA and claimed to be neither endorsing nor opposing the bill, in accordance with AA tradition. "But you must remember that as time passes in these hearings a great many AAs will be testifying as citizens, and they will be far more free to express their opinions."

"He encouraged other recovered alcoholics to testify 'as citizens' but in accordance with AA traditions, not to identify themselves in this public forum as members of AA," Olson wrote. Indeed, AA was barely mentioned during most of the testimony, though Hughes's legislative aide, a member of AA herself, later acknowledged that everyone who pushed for the bill's passage knew, as Wilson's comment suggested, that AA lay at the center of the policy.

Academy Award–winning actress Mercedes McCambridge was the most famous person to testify. Hughes, wanting a big star as part of the proceedings, had urged her to do so, though he warned, "Your appearance could hurt your career."

In his memoir he recalled, "The phone was silent for a moment. Then in that husky voice, 'OK, I'll do it.'"

She introduced herself as an alcoholic "of the protected Bel Air type," and testified, "As I sit here, scores of women like me are being arranged on slabs in morgues throughout this country with tickets tied to their toes that read 'Acute Alcoholism.'"

Looking over McCambridge's shoulder, Hughes's assistant Olson could see that "the statement she read from was marked like an actor's script, noting where to pause, where to raise your voice for emphasis, and so on."

"Nobody need die of this disease," McCambridge told the senators. "We are eminently salvageable. We are well worth the trouble. We are eminently equipped to enrich this world. We write poetry, we paint pictures, we compose music, we build bridges, we head corporations, we win coveted prizes for the world's greatest literature, and too often, too many of us die from our disease, not our sin, not our weakness."

When she was done, Senator Yarborough said, "Miss McCambridge, I vote you another Oscar, this time for public service."

The next day the AP reported, "A U.S. Senator, an Academy Award–winning actress, a judge and two clergymen turned a Senate hearing into a session of Alcoholics Anonymous."

Another round of public hearings was held in the Senate on May 21 and 25, 1970. Among those who testified were Peter Domick, US senator from Colorado; Luther A. Cloud, president of the National Council on Alcoholism; Maxwell Weisman, director of alcohol programs for the state of Maryland; Marvin A. Block, of the Committee on Alcoholism and Drug Dependence of the American Medical Association; Morris E. Chafetz, of Massachusetts General Hospital (and later the first director of the National Institute on Alcohol Abuse and Alcoholism); and Selden D. Bacon. The bill was passed unanimously by the Senate on August 10.

The bill would have to make it past President Nixon, who was thoroughly opposed to it. His intention was to not sign it, to let it die by pocket veto, though two of his cabinet members had recommended he veto it outright. But

R. Brinkley Smithers, Mann's wealthy supporter, started working his political connections. He recalled an old friend of his who was a close advisor of President Nixon: Don Kendall, who was then chairman of PepsiCo (Nixon had been Pepsi's corporate attorney during the years between his loss in the California governor's race and his win of the presidency). Kendall had become one of Nixon's closest advisors and would be instrumental in the administration's later efforts to overthrow Salvador Allende after his election as president of Chile. Smithers called Kendall, who was quickly convinced of the bill's merits and agreed to talk to the president.

One phone call, and Kendall moved the president to quietly sign the bill, which deadlines required him to do by New Year's Eve. Legend has it that he signed it on that last day of 1970, but the Nixon Presidential Library has no evidence that he did. According to one of Nixon's biographies, the president spent that night mixing martinis in the Executive Office Building for famed White House reporter Helen Thomas and other journalists.

Two years later, with Nixon's help, Kendall orchestrated the first trade deal between an American company and the Soviet Union—soda pop for vodka.

4 | 1970–1983: ZEITGEIST

Bill Wilson and the Science of Controlled Drinking

In the end, it wasn't alcohol that killed Bill Wilson. Even as Wilson testified for the Hughes Act, he was dying. Severely emphysemic from a lifetime of chain smoking, he dragged an oxygen tank around with him at all times, and he would joke with friends about whether he should have air or another cigarette. More often than not, he'd go with the smoke. He showed up to his last public appearance, at AA's 1970 convention in Miami, in a wheelchair, from which he rose to share just a few words. By the time President Nixon decided to sign the Hughes Act, Wilson was bedridden in his home just outside New York. The nurses' notes show that he asked several times for some whiskey—indeed, begged for it. This was the man who'd written in the Big Book, AA's bible, that a thorough and honest undertaking of the Twelve Steps would forever remove an alcoholic's desire to drink. Yet here he was, desperate for one last taste.

Though it surely wouldn't have made his condition any worse, his wife and nurses refused his request. He became enraged and demanded they give him a drink. But still they denied him, and he lay there dying sober for the sake of a dogma he had helped bring into the world and lamented. Years earlier, Wilson had written, "It is an historical fact that practically all groupings of men and women tend to become more dogmatic; their beliefs and practices harden and sometimes freeze." He called it "a natural and almost inevitable process," but warned that "dogma also has its liabilities. Simply because we

111

have convictions that work well for us, it becomes very easy to assume that we have all the truth. This isn't good dogma; it's very bad dogma. It could be especially destructive for us of AA to indulge in this sort of thing."

Throughout his life, Wilson had explicitly and repeatedly said that AA was never intended as a universal cure: "In no circumstances should members feel that Alcoholics Anonymous is the know-all and do-all of alcoholism"; "it would be a product of false pride to believe that Alcoholics Anonymous is a cure-all, even for alcoholism"; "AA has no monopoly on reviving alcoholics." And the Big Book, AA's basic text, states up front, "In all probability, we shall never be able to touch more than a fair fraction of the alcohol problem in all its ramifications."

Although there's no record of him weighing in on the controversy over the study by D. L. Davies showing that some alcoholics are able to return to moderate drinking, in the Big Book itself Wilson wrote that some problem drinkers may be able to do so:

> We have a certain type of hard drinker. He may have the habit badly enough to gradually impair him physically and mentally. It may cause him to die a few years before his time. If a sufficiently strong reason—ill health, falling in love, change of environment, or the warning of a doctor—becomes operative, this man can also stop or moderate, although he may find it difficult and troublesome and may even need medical attention.

As Wilson lay in his death bed, a pair of young scientists in Southern California were conducting an experiment that would validate his musings about hard drinkers and moderation and open up promising new directions for the treatment of alcoholism.

Mark Sobell had just completed a three-year fellowship toward a PhD in psychology at the University of California, Riverside when he was offered a job managing a research grant at Patton State Hospital in San Bernardino to conduct studies in aversion therapy. The researchers planned to videotape severe alcoholics getting drunk and then have them watch themselves while sober. The experiment would be conducted in a bar the hospital had built in a room in its basement and stocked with liquor confiscated by the state's alcohol commission. It was an incredible opportunity, and Sobell's partner and soon-to-be wife, Linda, then an undergraduate in psychology, joined the project. Early in the process, however, the hospital's video equipment broke down, and the couple sat idle with a staff of six.

As luck would have it, a staff member from the hospital's alcoholism ward came to them at that exact time seeking help with a patient. "I know as scientists you can talk some sense into him," the orderly said. "He tells me that he's going to learn to drink responsibly. He doesn't want to be abstinent and doesn't know any reason why he has to be abstinent. So I want you to tell him why."

"Gee, well, I'm sure you're right," Sobell, in an interview with me, recalled saying. At the time, he didn't know much about alcoholism, other than a sort of common wisdom that alcoholics can't drink in moderation, which he says he gleaned through "folklore."

He met with the patient, and the patient insisted: "I've tried abstinence, but I don't like it at all. I'm either going to die a drunk or I'm going to learn to control my drinking. Why do I have to stop?"

"That's a good question, and I'm embarrassed to say I don't know," Sobell replied. "I'll tell you what. We need to learn more about this field anyway. We're going to be hitting the literature. When I find out why you can't drink, I'll get back to you and tell you why."

He told his idle research team to go to the library and scour journals for a scientific basis for abstinence. They found nothing that definitively said why alcoholics need to quit. But they did find twenty-three studies dating back to the early 1940s revealing clear instances in which alcoholics had been able to switch to moderation. They discovered the controversy over the Davies report of the early 1960s, the mental gymnastics that proponents of the disease model went through to explain away Davies's findings, and Seltzer's claim that higher-ups had tried to coerce him to bury what he'd found.

This got the Sobells' inquiring minds churning. From the start, Mark Sobell had doubts about the efficacy of aversion training, but this new information led him to think in the opposite direction: perhaps alcoholics could be taught to drink in moderation.

The scientists gathered seventy patients who fit the definition of gamma alcoholics according to Jellinek's scale—"That is, prior to treatment they had all reported reaching a point where they were unable to control their drinking," Sobell explained, "and all had experienced some degree of physiological withdrawal symptoms due to the absence of alcohol." As a state facility,

Patton Hospital, which supplied the subjects for the study, was known as "the looney bin" and was, in Sobell's words, "a place to warehouse" drunks of the most extreme variety.

The Sobells' research team interviewed each subject and assigned each to either a treatment goal of abstinence or controlled drinking, whichever was considered most appropriate. Within each division, both the abstainers and the controlled drinkers, patients were randomly assigned to an experimental or control group.

Afterward, the team followed up with regularly scheduled surveys, asking "How many days since our last contact have you had anything to drink?" After a year, 85 percent of the controlled drinking subjects "functioned well"—meaning they had few or no days of binge drinking—compared to 32 percent of their control group. Among the abstinent group, 87 percent functioned well compared to 27 percent in the control group. In other words, the drinkers fared just as well as the nondrinkers. Their study had produced a scientific refutation of the conception of a disease for which the only cure is total abstinence.

The Sobells had no clue what kind of response their research would get. They felt lucky just to be able to do interesting research, and they hoped the scientific community would look favorably on their work. Little did they know that their fellow scientists were not the only ones who would take an interest in their work. They didn't know that there was an entire other community built around the issue of alcoholism that would receive their findings very differently.

"We had no idea of the traditional alcoholism field," Sobell said. "We were just interested in the science. We had no idea where things would go."

The National Institute of AA

Another young scientist who was entering the field at that time, Marsha Vannicelli, had finished graduate school at Tufts University just a year earlier when she was instantly catapulted to the highest level of alcoholism policy making in the United States. Upon graduation in 1970, she had received a training fellowship at Massachusetts General Hospital sponsored by the newly formed National Institute on Alcohol Abuse and Alcoholism, and while serving in that position, the NIAAA's newly appointed director, Morrie Chafetz, went looking, in the interest of diversity, for "a young woman" to serve on the institute's advisory council. Vannicelli's name came up, and she was appointed. Now a practicing therapist who specializes in treating addictions, she offers an array of treatment strategies, of which AA is just one.

What she most remembers is that the group was almost all male, with just two "token" women, herself and Marty Mann. "She represented AA," Vannicelli said, adding, "there were a number of people in recovery. I'm guessing about 80 percent of the people on the board were in recovery through AA."

Among the board members were James Kemper of Kemper Insurance and Thomas Pike, a prominent California Republican who, along with R. Brinkley Smithers, had worked behind the scenes to get Nixon to sign the bill creating the NIAAA. Other advisory council members included Peter Hutt, who had taken the question of alcoholism as a disease all the way to the Supreme Court and had written the legislation that created the NIAAA, and a Dr. F. Morris Lookout, who represented Native Americans. It was "primarily a rubber stamp committee," Vannicelli said, adding that at meetings she "looked active because I was always writing, but I was actually doing my clinical notes. I didn't want to be wasting my time."

But the council meeting notes show she spoke up on a number of occasions, most often to offer a counterpoint to the group's most outspoken proponents of AA, and these exchanges show how in its early years the newly created NIAAA operated as if it were a federalized extension of Mann's campaign to narrowly define alcoholism and to promote AA as its most effective cure. At the first of two all-day meetings in June 1972, Vannicelli argued in defense of grant proposals for research in the burgeoning field of "behavior modification," which the Sobells' controlled-drinking study had been a part of. Pike said these kinds of study proposals should be given "a very low priority," adding: "I am against it. The name of our business ought to be recovery here."

Chafetz dismissed them as "research fads."

But Vannicelli pushed back: "A lot of things we are looking at are also fads"—referring to various grant proposals on new trends in AA-based recovery. She'd come to the committee with an open mind, believing that "there doesn't have to be just one way" to address drinking problems. "There's more than one way to skin a cat," she said.

Pike talked over her. "Well-meaning scientists," he said, "take as a premise that alcoholism is a learned behavior. Ergo that it can be unlearned. Which in my humble judgment I think is much too narrow."

"In California we've seen a lot of experiments," he went on, referring perhaps to the Sobells' work: "One study paid drunks and tried to teach them, 'when you drink, drink like a gentleman.' If a person is truly an alcoholic, a compulsive, addictive drinker, then he has lost the ability ever to relearn the ability to drink, which these fellows seem to think you can do. That is pretty unscientific."

Though Chafetz seemed to agree, he closed the debate with a call for objectivity. "I would fight to the death to support grants that have been reviewed in a careful way, even if they don't fit into my preconceptions of alcoholism," he said. "If you don't do that, you get into a situation where we are perpetuating our own propaganda."

Pike would later write in his memoir that Chafetz was

a Harvard-trained psychiatrist. . . . A brilliant, but highly egocentric person who seemed to think he knew everything there was to know about alcoholism, he suffered the same myopic limitations which afflict so many of his colleagues in the mental health establishment. He was neither able to discern any mote in his own eye nor any deficiency in his own knowledge and understanding of alcoholism. This limitation is unfortunately shared by many professionals in medicine and psychiatry, and constitutes one of the major obstacles standing in the way of more effective collaboration on the treatment of alcoholism between the professionals and paraprofessionals.

In hindsight, the observation is as revealing of Pike and the community of AA promoters he hailed from as it is of Chafetz, because it shows their disdain for highly educated treatment proponents.

However, a discussion that dominated much of the next day's meeting, one in which Vannicelli participated much more extensively, revealed that perpetuating such propaganda about preconceptions of alcoholism drove the NIAAA's agenda in its early days.

The meeting began with a resolution offered by Pike:

Whereas Alcoholics Anonymous is recognized as one of the most successful treatment modalities for alcoholism ever developed in this country, the NIAAA hereby declares that: (1) its policy on all grant requests for treatment and community assistance programs is to require that AA cooperation and participation be sought to the maximum extent possible in all treatment programs; and, (2) that a statement to this effect be included—must be included—in all such grant requests, and (3) that AA, General Services Office, the NCA and other liaison members of this council, be notified of this policy with the request that their respective constituencies be so advised and that their cooperation be respectfully and earnestly solicited.

Mann immediately seconded it.

"What would be gained by this resolution?" Vannicelli asked after discussion began.

"I think a lot," Mann replied.

Pike said he was offering the resolution because he'd been looking at some projects in California—perhaps the Sobells' study—that "never have made any attempt to use AA and to me that is just like throwing good money, good resources, out the window, paying no attention to it."

"I don't see why you should start off with the Alcoholics Anonymous paragraph, because it still seems like you are leading to AA," Vannicelli argued. "I don't think you have anything to gain by that."

"I couldn't disagree with you more," Pike said. "There are several hundred thousand people that are sober from this, and they exist by bringing the recovery they got to other people. I don't think you have been involved for twenty-five years like I have."

"You are right. I haven't," Vannicelli said. "My question is, why does this council want to single out AA?"

Hutt pointed out that there were other untapped areas of expertise—local mental health workers, local volunteer groups. "I am troubled at the language of requiring that this be done," he said. "To require that AA be used, as good as it is, it troubles me because I think one of the things we are trying to do is open up, rather than to limit, the possibilities."

Chafetz agreed. "No one has greater respect for AA than I," he said, but "one of the things I find fault with AA is that the rest of us have used AA as an excuse not to get involved in this field. They have been a nice excuse for the medical profession" to not address alcoholism—the same argument Arthur Cain made almost ten years earlier in *Harper's*—"I have gone around and done surveys and heard the medical people say, of course we have a program in alcoholism, we send them to AA." He pointed out, too, that "AA is a threat to [the NIAAA] because legislators can say you don't need money, you have AA."

"This will make us look like an AA council," Vannicelli said.

"How could it?" Mann asked. "How could it?"

Vannicelli didn't respond.

"I am the only Indian present, and I am filled with a great deal of fear about what is taking place," Dr. Lookout said.

> AA has not been successful with the Indian alcoholic. I don't foresee Indian communities reaching out to AA because I have seen the over-zealous AAs, and I have seen a lot of good AAs, but by the same token I have seen an equal amount of bad AAs that I do not want to go out to and solicit help from. I think in their overzealousness, they tend to take over the Indian program, and I think this takes us away from Indian control and Indian initiative. So I am definitely opposed to this.

Similarly another member recalled a recent visit to a treatment center in Arkansas where the program was "highly oriented to AA" but the population was predominantly black and Hispanic, and when introduced to AA groups, the members said, "They went one time, ran away. They didn't want anything to do with it."

The advisory council didn't resolve the matter that day, instead tabling it to their September meeting, at which neither Pike nor Vannicelli were present. In the interim, NIAAA staff combed the files and queried their grant recipients and were able to show that they already had a policy of including AA in their initiatives and that the overwhelming majority of people working under NIAAA grants were affiliated with AA. After this staff presentation, Hutt remarked that it was essentially "a reiteration of policy, a confirmation of existing policy."

After a brief discussion of minor wording issues, they voted to adopt the resolution with just a few, insignificant tweaks. In doing so, they formally brought the full force of the federal government behind Marty Mann's campaign. With tens of millions of dollars to spend, the NIAAA's formation and early years of operation would spark explosive growth in the alcoholism treatment industry, in which AA was invariably the sole course of remedy. The institute would also enrich Mann's organization, the NCA, and its affiliates with millions in grants to carry on the work that Mann had struggled to carry out since the early days of her sobriety in the late 1940s.

Rabble-Rousing

In the mid-1970s, the NIAAA became flush with an inordinate amount of money. During its first couple years of existence, Nixon, still fuming about its creation, had impounded its appropriations, along with money earmarked for scores of other domestic programs approved by the Democrat-controlled Congress. After a couple years of fighting, a judge ordered all the back funds released at once, flooding the new agency with more than $800 million that had to be spent immediately. Limited in staff size, it used grants and contracts to drain the funds quickly. Mann's group got a whopping $6.9 million to develop new local councils and establish occupational alcoholism programs in ten cities, and the institute went hunting for groups that might use the many millions more it had to give, giving little direction in how to use them other than to "get involved." Chafetz called these "rabble rousing programs," due to their aim of changing public perception about alcohol and its attendant problems.

There was one area, however, that the NIAAA's most vocal constituency wasn't keen on funding: scientific research. The institute did have a research division, but the bulk of its money went toward treatment programs and public relations. A big reason for this was that these were activists who helped create the NIAAA—anonymous alcoholics who'd recovered through AA and their family and friends—who didn't want the institute to spend money researching alcoholism and varieties of treatment. They knew what alcoholism was, and they had a cure for it—AA. They wanted its efficacy to be proven, and they wanted to spread the AA message across the country.

To carry out this mission, the NIAAA hired the prestigious ad agency Grey-North. One of the resulting ads, called "The Plague," featured eerie music playing behind a narrator calmly asking,

> What if a terrible disease came to our land and millions of us got very sick? And what if that disease killed eighty-six thousand of us every year and still kept growing like a plague? What would we do?

Would we close our eyes, not see the disease, never talk about it? Would we lock up some of the sick ones where we could not see or hear them? Would we call them bad names, tell them to stop being sick, because their disease was disgusting and immoral? We would call that disease . . . alcoholism, wouldn't we?

On the treatment side, the vast coffers funded programs that employed the Minnesota Model, and as a result AA very quickly became institutionalized across the United States. Judges could now force problem drinkers to go to AA. More and more insurance companies, negotiating with corporate clients that employed millions of workers, followed Kemper's lead and began covering treatment, so the number of treatment facilities mushroomed. Employers could now send their hard-drinking workers to treatment centers, some costing six figures a month, fully covered by insurance, where they'd be taught to live the AA way. These were very profitable for hospitals and clinics; following the model pioneered in Minnesota, which had been replicated across the country, recovery counselors didn't need graduate degrees—and as such could be paid less—and alcoholism treatment didn't require expensive medical equipment.

Amid all these changes, Hughes, the man whose legislation had set them into motion, lamented what he was seeing. Despite being on a shortlist to run for president in 1972 and appearing destined for a long career in national politics, he walked away. One day he went into the meditation room he'd created in the Capitol and knelt and prayed as he did every day, when a thought struck him. "Was it true that I really wanted to serve Christ in every possible way?" he would recall. "Yes, my soul cried out. Yes!" to which the thought in his mind replied: *Then give up your position as senator and serve me full time.* He announced he wouldn't seek reelection in 1974.

Late in his one and only term as a senator, he gave a speech at the North American Congress on Alcohol and Drug Problems in San Francisco where he likened the campaign for a national alcoholism treatment system to "waging a war. And, like any war, the waging of the conflict affects those who participate, often in unforeseen ways.

"We have, in effect, a new civilian army that has now become institutionalized. The alcohol and drug industrial complex is not as powerful as its military-industrial counterpart, but nonetheless there are some striking similarities."

He asked,

Are we truly interested in helping human beings in need, or is our involvement a device for massaging our egos by regimenting people in the guise of helping them? Do we feel ourselves beginning to surrender to the false glory of bureaucratic empire building?

Have we become so hidebound with our own methods and approaches to the problem that we can't fairly consider alternative methods? Do we feel ourselves at any point drifting into the carping criticism syndrome—the stage where we can sit back and find fault with the creative workers in the field, split hairs over the language of research findings, and wrangle fruitlessly over issues that don't make an ounce of difference to the sick person who is supposed to be the beneficiary of all this effort?

Post politics, Hughes devoted himself to Christ, helping both porn king Larry Flynt and Watergate mastermind Chuck Colson to get born again (he even starred as himself in the movie version of Colson's salvation). He founded a network of treatment facilities, served on the board of the NCA, and worked as a consultant with R. Brinkley Smithers of the Smithers Foundation.

A New Breed of Alcoholism Scientists

Despite the lowly status of research initiatives at the NIAAA in its early years, the institute did devote some money to scientific inquiry. The biggest investment was for a study to be conducted by the RAND Corporation, a nonprofit think tank based in California, to look at outcomes from treatment facilities supported by the institute. Chafetz was well aware that his new organization had a mandate from Congress to not only address the problem of alcoholism but to show results, so he made the assessment inquiry a top priority.

The NIAAA offered smaller grants for science community researchers as well, and Mark and Linda Sobell won one, for $4,900 to conduct a two-year follow-up on their controlled drinking study. This study revealed even better results than the first one, showing that "subjects treated with a controlled drinking goal functioned significantly better than their respective control subjects on a variety of measures, including drinking behavior. Differences between subjects treated with a non-drinking goal and their control subjects did not retain statistical significance during the second-year of follow-up."

The Sobells published their findings in the journal *Behaviour Research and Therapy* in 1976, and the response among the scientific community was positive. To the couple's delight, they received an invitation that year to present their findings at a symposium hosted by the Addiction Research Foundation in Toronto, then and now a renowned center for the field. The Sobells viewed the opportunity as a tremendous honor, a chance to associate with "people we looked up to as real leaders in behavioral research." They were soon recruited by Vanderbilt University to join its faculty, which thrilled these two alumni of the University of California, Riverside, which was at the time not known as a top research institution. Despite their inauspicious beginnings, the two were rising quickly at a young age in the growing field of behavior therapy and alcoholism and addiction treatment.

As word of the Sobells' research spread, other young scientists took notice and followed in their footsteps. One, William Miller, came across the Sobells' study while working as an intern at a VA hospital in Milwaukee, during a summer break from grad school. The director of the hospital had given him freedom to look around to decide which wards and programs interested him. He stopped by the alcoholism unit. At the time, alcoholism wasn't a desirable field for psychology students to pursue. "It was like, why would you want to spend your time doing that?" Miller recalled. But to his surprise, he felt drawn to the field and enjoyed talking with the patients. Maybe, he thought, alcoholism research offered a way for him to make a real impact on society.

At the VA hospital, Miller saw mostly difficult cases, severely dependent alcoholics who'd lost friends, family, and homes. He learned that the conventional wisdom was that these patients had no real choice but to drink until they got so sick and their lives got so miserable that they finally were ready to quit. But this didn't seem right to him. "It seemed to me you could do something to help these people before they get to this point," he said.

That "a-ha" moment marked a turning point in his academic and professional career; he reworked his dissertation plan to study how to develop ways to address problem drinking earlier. Alcoholism was such an unexplored field that no one in his department at the University of Oregon had much interest in it, much less any real knowledge about it. One faculty member had done some smoking research, so the professor agreed to be Miller's advisor. The school's internal review board wasn't quite sure what to make of his work;

one member, who was a pastor, commented that Miller shouldn't be doing the kind of research he was doing, that he should be doing Jungian therapy.

He came to see alcoholism as something akin to diabetes, where there are numerous ways to intervene earlier in patients' lives. "It was moderation under the name of controlled drinking," he said, explaining that early research.

Unlike the Sobells, Miller discovered early on that his interests were out of step with the larger alcoholism recovery community. "At the time, it was extremely controversial because of the disease concept of alcoholism," he said. "During the process, one local fellow accused me of being a murderer."

But he sensed that he and other young scientists he'd met at conferences around the country were onto something big and important. "There was a seismic shift taking place," he said.

Decadence in the Field of Alcoholism

The spending frenzy continued at the NIAAA. To Marsha Vannicelli, who served on the institute's advisory council, some of the expenditures seemed extravagant. In particular she remembers a two-day event the institute put on in collaboration with the NCA, Marty Mann's organization. It was held in a lush convention hotel ballroom in Washington, DC, with top-chef catering and a full orchestra.

Soon members of Congress took notice, most notably Senator William Proxmire, a Democrat from Wisconsin, who singled out an NIAAA grant in 1976 for his Golden Fleece Award, for "spending millions of dollars to find out if drunk fish are more aggressive than sober fish; if young rats are more likely than adult rats to drink booze in order to reduce anxiety; and if rats can be systematically turned into alcoholics." Milking the pun potential for all it was worth, his news release read, "NIAAA seems to be testing what it means to be 'stewed to the gills.' Or perhaps they want to understand what is really behind the expression, 'drinks like a fish.'"

Fiscal red flags had been raised before then. In early 1974, columnist Jack Anderson reported that Chafetz and several of his top aides had billed the government for a five-day stay in Palm Springs in March 1974 and that he'd spent tax dollars to charter a plane to Alaska for two salmon fishing trips with executives at an advertising firm. The expenditure alone was enough to raise eyebrows, but Chafetz allowed the executives to be reimbursed for the trip, a case of double-billing, and then turned around and approved renewal of the agency's $1.4 million contract.

Chafetz, who would resign in 1975 amid this controversy, agreed to an internal investigation of the institute's contracts, and the review found that some of the organization's reviewers of grant applications "had potential conflicts of interest in that they were later employed by the grants which they recommended for approval."

The grants in question were for the NCA, Mann's organization. Totaling several million dollars, they paid for activities the NCA had been doing since its inception under the auspices of Yale in the 1940s. One was "to effect prevention and education by improving the distribution of educational materials relating to alcoholism and alcohol abuse" through "television, radio, newspapers, trade publications" and "utilizing agencies such as AA and Al-Anon." Another was to "mobilize top business and union leadership to volunteer for task forces to influence corporations and unions to adopt and promote employee alcoholism programs." Perhaps most egregiously, one NCA grant, for $1.45 million, was awarded with a goal of helping to create more local affiliates for the NCA itself. The NCA was, of course, a lobbying organization. Indeed, it had lobbied hard for the very institution that was now funneling money its way. NCA officials denied the funds would go directly to lobbying efforts, and the investigators conceded the difficulty of proving precisely how the money would be spent, concluding: "The lobbying issue is difficult to confront with an organization whose purpose no doubt is partly exactly that."

The investigators found the NCA's records to be "strikingly incomplete" and that at least two members of the NIAAA National Advisory Council had "personal/professional" interest in the NCA, but the advisory council's minutes didn't show that they recused themselves from the discussion or voting. The investigators found that the office of the institute director "purposely ignored the usual review procedures and frustrated or circumvented the usual safeguards" to ensure that the NCA received its grant, that he and fellow leaders were "highly active" in marshaling grant applications toward approval, and that they "sacrificed historically acceptable standards of public administration for speed and expediency in order to fund applications of questionable quality." In conclusion, they declared: "The objectivity of grant review procedures, the stewardship of NIAAA monitoring, and the evaluation methods employed by the grantees were, with few exceptions, seriously deficient."

Even supporters of Mann's organization frowned on the direction it had taken. "NCA was a wonderful organization," wrote Nancy Olson, aide to Senator Harold Hughes. "But after passage of the Hughes Act, they became addicted to federal money and soon had more than 50 percent of their budget from federal funds."

"When alcoholism acquired disease status, both medically and legally, alcoholism programs suddenly seemed less tainted in Washington's budget and appropriations circle," wrote Jay Lewis, a reporter and columnist for the *Alcoholism Report*, a trade publication. "This has proven to be a mixed blessing," attracting "those whose devotion to the cause of assisting the nation's alcoholics can be most charitably described as hastily acquired. We should probably not be surprised that money for alcoholism programs is sometimes finding its way into the hands of angle shooters and other modern counterparts of the old-time purveyors of snake oil."

And speaking at an NCA forum years later in Seattle, Peter Barton Hutt, author of the bill that created the NIAAA, told the audience they were in a "period of decadence in the field," which had become "as addicted to federal funds as the alcoholic is addicted to alcohol. . . . It has begun to concentrate on its own self-survival, not on help."

Disputing Science

Shortly before Morrie Chafetz resigned amid all the scandal at his agency, he received the results of the first major scientific study the institute had funded, the assessment by the RAND Corporation of the efficacy of federally funded treatment programs. The data showed that eighteen months after being released from treatment, a full twenty-two percent of the patients had become "normal drinkers." Moreover, the study revealed that

> the majority of improved clients are either drinking moderate amounts of alcohol—but at levels far below what could be described as alcoholic drinking—or engaging in alternating periods of drinking and abstention . . . this finding suggests the possibility that for some alcoholics moderate drinking is not necessarily a prelude to full relapse and that some alcoholics can return to moderate drinking with no greater chance of relapse than if they abstained.

Meanwhile, they found that "only a relatively small number" of patients went on to become "long-term abstainers," which was the goal of their treatment.

This was a surprise even to the report's authors, who acknowledged in the preface that they were "aware that some of the findings of the present study—particularly the finding that some alcoholics appear to return to patterns of normal drinking—may be controversial in some quarters."

Chafetz revealed the results at a meeting of the National Advisory Council on Alcohol Abuse and Alcoholism on St. Patrick's Day 1975. Facing a crowd stacked heavily in favor of the AA concept of alcoholism as a disease, which emphatically concludes that it's impossible for alcoholics to drink in moderation, he tried to put a positive spin on the results, pointing out that they showed that 70 percent of treatment patients recover in one way or another. He argued that using abstinence as a sole criterion for recovery skews results and that by calculating a broad range of outcomes, this study showed improvement at every level. He told council members, "You better get rid of your favorite therapies," because the findings showed that it didn't really matter which treatment was used. "The treatment approach is less important than the fact that you . . . listen to the person and find out what they are looking for.

"Some of these people show that they have long periods where they have taken some alcohol and have still not gone down the tubes," Chafetz said. But he quickly added, "So that I don't get killed by some of my friends, I am not advocating that people drink when they have alcohol problems. But I think it is absolutely the most hopeful kind of data to share with the American public. If anything, it reaffirms what we have been saying, that alcoholism is a very treatable illness."

The council meeting minutes reveal a measured response by pro-AA members of the board, perhaps suggesting a level of shock. Mann merely asked if the study could be continued for another eighteen months in order to allow for three-year follow-up. Katherine Pike, who'd replaced her husband Thomas on the council, said, "I think it is a very interesting report and I regret that we only got it last night and have not had the time to absorb it fully."

But, in the words of Hughes's former aide, Nancy Olson, "The report started a war that continues to this day." She said this in the 1990s, but it would still apply now.

Thomas Pike, then a member of the RAND Corporation's board, "fought like a tiger" with the authors of the report, urging them to repudiate it and pressuring RAND's leadership to spike the findings. When they didn't, he resigned from the board. His wife, Katherine, wrote to the NIAAA's deputy director that by including imbibers of small amounts of alcohol under the umbrella term of "recovery," the report

> ignores the widely accepted premise that abstinence is an essential requirement . . . to include those people who report consumption of less than one ounce a day provides support for the few researchers who have undertaken to demonstrate that the treated alcoholic can return to controlled drinking. In my opinion, based on my years of extensive experience, this is a dangerous position for NIAAA. Alcoholics notably try to limit their consumption, and many die in the attempt.

More than a year of backroom fighting occurred—with NIAAA leaders facing serious pressure to suppress the findings—before the report was released in 1976, at which point, the attacks against it escalated. One line of attack was the researchers' use of self-reporting by former patients of the treatment centers, because, in the sarcastic words of one of the report's authors: "they're all liars. Except when they go to AA and say they've abstained for three months, somehow they're not." Chafetz later said on the TV show *Crossfire*, "I refused to suppress the publication of the report—paternalism is even more destructive than alcoholism," adding that the results were just common sense: "For a person who lives in a drinking society, to think he must stop drinking entirely to control his alcoholism problem may discourage him from seeking treatment until he's really down in the dumps."

When the report finally came out, Mann's group quickly called a press conference to denounce it, calling it "dangerous," and warning: "It will cause an awful lot of people to die." The executive director of the San Francisco chapter of the NCA told the *Berkeley Gazette*,

> I have taken some of the "experiments" to the hospital and watched them die. . . . There is nothing in the world an alcoholic wants more than to be able to do that [controlled drinking]. Somehow they want to be told that. I am a walking example of this. I made nine trips in one year to a recovery facility because I couldn't accept the fact that I could not drink the way other people did.

Even the NIAAA, for its part, redressed the facts with a lie, declaring that the study proved that "those who were dependent on alcohol cannot go back to normal drinking." Ernie Noble, the institute's new director, lamented the report's release and swore he'd keep a "careful eye on such research activities in the future."

But future research only served to further validate the findings.

In 1980, the NIAAA conducted a four-year follow-up on the RAND report that confirmed and extended the original results: nearly 20 percent of the patients reported drinking without problems or symptoms of dependence, and fewer than 10 percent managed to maintain total abstinence. "When we examined longer time periods and multiple points in time," the researchers wrote, "we found a great deal of change in individual status, with some persons continuing to improve, some persons deteriorating, and most moving back and forth between relatively improved and unimproved statuses."

New Directions

After Hughes stepped down, Senator William Hathaway (D-ME) took over his position as chair of the committee overseeing the NIAAA. Not long into his tenure, the *Alcoholism Report* reported on January 9, 1976, that Hathaway said, "We don't really know whether alcoholism is in fact a 'disease.'" He continued: "Now, I realize that federal law specifically calls alcoholism a 'disease.' But that law was written by politicians not by medical researchers. It might well be that one of the problems in alcoholism is too much politics and too little research. As Winston Churchill once said: 'One easy catchword can destroy two generations of creative thought.'"

Changes were brewing within the NIAAA as well. After Chafetz's resignation amid allegations of misuse of funds, Dr. Earnest Noble took over. He wanted to steer more of the institute's resources into research at the expense of AA-based treatment centers and PR campaigns promoting the disease concept of alcoholism. Moreover, he had a mandate from the newly elected President Jimmy Carter to shake things up.

It wasn't that the new administration was anti-AA. Carter's health secretary, Joseph Califano Jr., had worked on alcoholism policy as a staffer in the Johnson White House—indeed, he'd helped write the speech in which Johnson declared alcoholism a disease—and he was very supportive of AA. Early in his tenure as secretary, he visited AA's headquarters in New York and was presented with the two millionth copy of the Big Book. He pledged "continuing and close cooperation" with AA. "I am asking all of our federally supported treatment programs to seek out AA organizations in the areas they serve, and to work with them so that recovering alcoholics leaving our programs will be fully aware of the support AA stands ready to give."

But Carter had run on a fiscally conservative platform, and the administration's sights were set on programs that had been shown to be wasteful, as the NIAAA had been several years earlier with its fishing junkets and millions in grants steered toward the NCA, the very organization that had lobbied for the NIAAA's existence. So Califano and his staff zeroed in on the institute's grant program for reform. "It was sort of a wasteland," Califano said of the NIAAA in an interview with me. "No one paid any attention to them. Nobody ever talked to them. They were sort of out in the wilderness."

At the NIAAA's advisory council meeting in March 1978, members discussed a proposed new procedure for reviewing programs that would receive federal grants. The new procedure would move the process for initial review of grant programs from the NIAAA to another federal agency, the Alcohol, Drug Abuse, and Mental Health Administration, or ADAMHA. Before discussion began, Noble cautioned, "There are always strong feelings in the area of alcoholism, but I would hope that our minds rule over our hearts."

Dozens of people crowded into the meeting room to speak out against the new measures, most of them affiliated with programs that had received grants. Luther Cloud, president of the NCA, read a statement that he and his colleagues were "concerned and dismayed" that the proposal "does little more than diminish, if not negate, a focus on alcoholism programming. We strongly urge this administration to recognize the alcoholism field and involve its principals in policymaking decisions affecting alcoholism programming." Such a move, he warned, would be "inadvisable and unacceptable" and "would deprive the NIAAA of its congressional mandate."

The Hughes Act had brought more than $1 billion into the alcoholism field over six years, several million of these dollars going to the NCA itself, so it's easy to see why the group would resist a change in policy. But there was something deeper at play here. The shift in leadership meant not only a change in granting procedure but also a dramatic directional change for the institute.

Noble sought to change it into more of a scientific organization and less of a propagandistic one, and he quickly succeeded. "We were able to double the research budget for the Institute," he said in a later interview. "We established nine alcohol research centers throughout the country."

He believed that the most important thing to do was to build a clear "understanding what this arcane disorder called alcoholism is all about," even if "people might not be pleased with all of the research results."

Subsequent directors shared his priorities, though it was a struggle to get them implemented. Robert Niven, who served as director of the NIAAA during the administration of President Ronald Reagan, recalled an agency that was still in transition, so he aimed to strengthen support for the institute's research mission in Congress and the White House, where officials, influenced by alcoholism advocates, "had mixed feelings about whether NIAAA should be involved in research," he later explained.

> They saw funding for research gradually increase, whereas funding for treatment services declined. That caused some animosity and skepticism toward NIAAA in Congress and among the non research constituency. However, we were able to overcome these negative perceptions, to strengthen our research activities, to increase our budget, and to attract more top-quality researchers.

Still, the change from being an agency modeled after Mann's NCA and a federal research entity came slowly. Speaking in the late 1990s, ten years after taking over from Niven as director of the NIAAA, Lauren Archer admitted that a top

> challenge for the future is to erase the old public misconception that although research may be very nice, we basically already know how to treat alcoholism effectively—all we have to do is get patients to attend AA meetings or therapy. In reality, however, it is quite the opposite. Alcoholism treatment only has limited effectiveness; many patients either do not receive treatment, do not like the treatment they receive, or relapse eventually.

War on Science

The NIAAA's move toward science would seem to have offered considerable opportunities for Mark and Linda Sobell and the growing cadre of addiction scientists who were following in their footsteps. Indeed their careers were very much on the upswing. In 1979, the couple got recruited away from Vanderbilt by the esteemed Addiction Research Foundation in Toronto, where they had been invited to speak earlier in their careers, and it appeared as though their careers had reached a pinnacle. Then in February 1982, the foundation's president suddenly called them into her office for a meeting. When they arrived, they saw the head of human resources was also in attendance, so they assumed the meeting would be about a person they had fired recently.

Instead the president posed a shocking question: "Do you know anything about a paper that's supposedly going to be in *Science* that would ruin your careers and possibly even take down this center?"

The article's lead author was Mary Pendery, a California psychologist, treatment center director, and outspoken champion of AA, who had shared a draft of the article with some associates, one of whom gave a copy to the Sobells after they learned of its existence. The article was worse than they'd expected. With two colleagues, Pendery claimed to have tracked down a number of the Sobells' subjects and to have conducted a follow-up study to show that those who'd undergone the controlled-drinking training had fared much worse than the Sobells had reported, that four out of the twenty controlled-drinking patients had died, two of them from excessive drinking.

The couple hired a lawyer and began a back and forth with the editors at the journal, delaying publication of the article. "It would've been better if we'd just let them publish it as it was," Sobell said of the piece. "The original was so bad, we would've hit them like a hydrogen bomb."

In the interim, Pendery and her associates leaked another draft to the press, feeding a flurry of news reports. Irving Maltzman, one of Pendery's coauthors, was quoted in the *New York Times* as saying of the Sobells' report, "Beyond any reasonable doubt, it's fraud." The CBS newsmagazine *60 Minutes* broadcast a segment by Harry Reasoner and producer Don Hewitt called "The Sobell Experiment." The Sobells refused to cooperate with the show. "What became very important to us, largely because we knew we were being wrongfully attacked, was to maintain our dignity and not get down in the mud and grovel with the other side," Linda Sobell later explained in an interview. The segment's producer, Hewitt, had interviewed someone who'd worked on the study who pointed out that the control group had a much higher mortality rate—50 percent higher. "We know that," Hewitt told him, according to his account to the Sobells. "But that's not the story."

"For several years, *60 Minutes* had been our favorite program," Sobell said, but now its producers were personally attacking the couple: "They told us the reason they called it 'The Sobell Experiment' was because we hadn't cooperated with them and they wanted to punish us."

Others in the field who knew the Sobells' work were aghast. "That was terrible," said Marsha Vannicelli. "I stopped watching *60 Minutes* after that. I always loved it, but in that report I saw what yellow journalism it is."

The climax of the segment was a shot in which Reasoner walked through a cemetery and paused by the grave of one of the study's subjects. What he didn't mention was that the person had died (of drowning while intoxicated) eleven years after the study—and just a couple of months after going through a traditional twenty-eight-day AA-based treatment program.

When *Science* published the article soon thereafter, its editors refused to allow the Sobells to write a response in the same issue, allowing only a two-hundred-word letter to the editor that would run in a later issue and would be subject to edits to which the Sobells wouldn't be privy. "A respectable journal would've solicited a simultaneous rebuttal," Sobell said. Instead, the pair opted to publish their response in the journal *Behaviour Research and Therapy*.

Others in the field came to their defense. "Most amazing is that the Pendery et al. paper was published with no information of the subjects who received the other forms of treatment," wrote Kelly Brownell, a professor of psychology and neuroscience at Duke University.

> Problems among the controlled-drinking subjects simply cannot be interpreted in the absence of data on the other groups. Even if the general outcome among controlled-drinking subjects was unfavorable, it could have been positive in a comparative manner if the other subjects did more poorly. This is tantamount to saying that a treatment for cancer is not useful if 80 percent of the patients do not survive. If the next best form of treatment yields a survival rate of only 10 percent, the treatment in question looks good in comparison.

Meantime, at the Sobells' request, the Addiction Research Foundation commissioned an independent investigation of the couple's research. ("The foundation knew what was going on," Sobell said. "They saw it as an attack on science in the addiction field.") The initial inquiry came to be known as the Dickens Committee inquiry, after its chair, law professor Bernard Dickens, and it consisted of distinguished senior scholars not involved in alcohol research. At the Sobells' first meeting with the committee, they were informed that they would be presumed guilty until proven otherwise. The committee spent five months investigating, and they met often with the Sobells, who gave them full access to their comprehensive archived data.

Mark Sobell told me that Linda obsessively files everything. "If a person in the study sent us a Christmas card, she would staple it to the envelope it came in and put it in a three-ring binder," he said. She'd stuffed a footlocker with receipts, lab notes, phone records, tape recordings, everything. In fact, the pair had intended to get rid of the stuff before they moved to Canada in the late '70s, but they were too busy to sort through it, so they loaded it on the moving trucks along with everything else they owned. Once in Toronto, their busy schedules continued, so the documents lay in cold storage, as if waiting to be used in their defense.

After five months, the Dickens Committee came back with its verdict, a 123-page report that declared a "clear and unequivocal" conclusion: "The Committee finds there to be no reasonable cause to doubt the scientific or personal integrity of either Dr. Mark Sobell or Dr. Linda Sobell."

Likewise, the lead investigator of a separate inquiry requested by Congress stated in a letter to the Sobells:

> Based upon my review of evidence, I have concluded that there is no evidence to support the allegation that your study was based upon fallacious, falsified or otherwise invented data. The correlation between your notes of contacts with patients, your phone logs and the tape recordings of those contacts have convinced me that your report of the study was made in good faith.

"Pendery was on a witch hunt, but there was no witch to be found," said Reid Hester, a clinical psychologist who closely followed the situation.

Several years after the controversy, Pendery was murdered by a drunk lover who had been treated in a hospital treatment facility where she worked.

Compared to the earlier press coverage, the investigations' exonerations received little attention and no mention from CBS News. While the Sobells' careers remained intact—they're now distinguished faculty at Nova Southeastern University in Fort Lauderdale—this very high-profile smear campaign would greatly curtail the impact their research and that of other scientists like them would have on people who struggle with drinking problems.

"American professionals who advocate any alternative to abstinence are likely to be (and have been) attacked as naïve fools, unwitting murderers, or perhaps themselves alcoholics denying their own disease," William Miller, a leading researcher at the Center on Alcoholism, Substance Abuse, and Addictions at the University of New Mexico, lamented in 1986. "And the controversy regarding the Sobell and Sobell study is likely to discourage future U.S. research on this topic for some time to come."

5 | 1983–1999: SUPPRESSED ALTERNATIVE

Blinkered

"Blinkered." That's the word William Miller used to describe the American alcoholism and addiction treatment community after he'd taken a sabbatical in Europe in 1982 to observe treatment communities abroad. It's a British term, he wrote in a reflective essay after his trip:

> It refers to the "blinkers" worn by a horse (which we would call blinders), designed to keep the animal looking straight ahead, eliminating distraction by events occurring in the world around it and preventing that animal from being frightened or confused by these occurrences. From my perspective as a temporary outsider, I find that "blinkered" is an accurate description of the American alcoholism community.

After some time in other countries, he could see more clearly how his colleagues had abandoned "scientific skepticism, respect for data, and theoretical eclecticism to worship at the idols of the 'traditional disease conception' of alcoholism," especially when *Alcoholism Magazine* published during his trip a testimonial by an American psychologist "who proudly confesses his personal denunciation of his scientific training in order to embrace the singleminded abstinence model."

But what surprised him most on his travels was to learn the extent to which he himself was blinkered as well. As a leading scholar in the growing community of behavioral scientists who sought innovative treatment of alcoholism in the States—and more specifically as an advocate for controlled drinking strategies—he considered himself something of a radical. But during a series of lectures in the United Kingdom, he "was astounded to find that my ideas which are seen as so heretical in America were regarded as quite noncontroversial, if not a bit old-fashioned. Indeed in Britain controlled drinking is a widely accepted phenomenon, and is regarded not as heresy but as a reasonable goal for some problem drinkers."

The problem with the American treatment system as he saw it was its "insistence that alcoholism is a disease." He didn't necessarily take issue with the use of the word, he wrote, "for as Jellinek recognized long ago that term is sufficiently vague as to be almost meaningless. A disease is whatever the medical profession chooses to proclaim a disease. Rather what seems patently absurd is the assertion that alcoholism is *a* disease; *one* syndrome."

He called America's treatment system a "powerful zeitgeist," one that dangerously lumps together all walks of problem drinkers into one diagnosis, a made-up disease created in the image of men and women who'd suffered the worst iterations of alcoholism. The zeitgeist's power had come not only from the convictions of its practitioners but from a burgeoning billion-dollar addiction treatment industry. Prior to the creation of the NIAAA, programs using the AA-based Minnesota Model had multiplied slowly, mostly by word of mouth, championed by members of AA and by the NCA's local organizing committees. For the most part, alcoholics still got shipped off to state psychiatric hospitals or were locked up in jail, if they were dealt with at all. But with the creation of an entire new federal agency devoted to alcoholism, with millions of dollars to spend, these programs proliferated rapidly. In its first ten years of existence, the NIAAA spent about $1 billion on this expansion, developing AA-based alcoholism services at the community level, according to Nancy Olson, the aide to the senator whose bill had made this public investment possible. This created a national network of treatment facilities, essentially codifying twelve-step recovery as America's alcoholism treatment policy.

"The growth of the overall field was staggering," psychologist William L. White wrote in *Slaying the Dragon: The History of Addiction Treatment and Recovery in America*. "The modern treatment industry grew from a handful of programs in the 1950s to 2,400 programs in 1977, to 6,800 in 1987, and to 9,057 in 1991." Increasingly these were private, for-profit enterprises, and they were very expensive, upwards of $25,000 for a monthlong stay.

In addition to the federal government's $1 billion subsidy via the NIAAA, the field was enjoying a capital influx from the private sector as well, with more and more insurers following Kemper Insurance's lead and offering treatment services to their clients. After Kemper had begun offering coverage in 1962, a handful of other companies—Hartford, Prudential, Blue Cross—started doing so, too. Then, in the 1980s, a little more than a decade into the NIAAA's existence, it became standard operating procedure to offer such coverage as more and more clients demanded treatment and state legislatures passed bills requiring it.

A study conducted jointly by the NIAAA and the National Institute on Drug Abuse in 1987 tallied 5,791 alcoholism treatment units in the country, among them 1,401 private for-profit treatment facilities—a quadrupling of such concerns since the early 1980s. When the NIAAA did another survey in 1993, it found that "more than 700,000 people receive alcohol treatment on any given day."

In this time of incredible growth, Hazelden developed a means by which to bring in more patients—the family intervention. As with the Minnesota Model it pioneered, this tactic was appropriated by treatment centers around the country. Officials at these facilities would work with concerned friends and family members of people with drinking problems to come together as a group and confront the loved one who was drinking too much. Often these came with an ultimatum: either get help now or say goodbye to their relationships. Before these meetings were staged, the families and treatment centers would reserve a bed for the recipient of the intervention, so he or she could be whisked away for the twenty-eight-day cure. These centers treated more than 350,000 patients.

"In this climate," White observed, "alcoholics and addicts became less people in need of treatment and more a crop to be harvested for their financial value." These programs were, and still are, highly profitable. Alcoholics don't require expensive, state-of-the-art equipment or cutting-edge drugs still under patent for their treatment. They didn't even need doctors. The nation had followed Minnesota's lead by making an exception for care providers in treatment centers and allowing them to be employed without advanced degrees. "A workforce had to be created—and created quickly," White wrote.

An incredible variety of people began working as alcoholism and drug abuse counselors without regard to their education, their training, or the stability of their personal recovery from addiction. In 1970, there were only six training programs in the entire country, and the requirements for certification were generally at least two years' sobriety, one year of counseling experience, and passage of a test on alcoholism knowledge. The NIAAA developed its own accrediting program during the 1970s, but the demand for counselors was far greater than what these accrediting agencies could churn out.

"There was no pool of educated and trained people willing or available to fill all the newly created positions," wrote White. "The answer to this dilemma was often the recruitment and cursory training of recovering people to work as outreach workers, house managers, detox technicians, 'patient counselors,' 'senior alcoholic patients,' 'AA counselors,' rehabilitation aides, or community educators."

And why not? Because the treatment was almost entirely rooted in AA, medical knowledge or training in psychology wasn't much needed. "In such programs, the recovering alcoholic hired as counselor was expected to be a walking tape recording of the AA recovery message," White explained, adding that "it was not unusual" for patients "still in treatment [to be] recruited into entry level employment. One day someone was a client in treatment; the next day he or she was employed in the same program."

The Anti-Intervention

While William Miller was on sabbatical in Europe, he made an "unexpected" discovery that would ultimately become one of the most effective ways to help people with drinking problems—unexpected because what he discovered was something he was already doing.

He spent some of his overseas time giving lectures in Norway, where the director asked him if he would also be willing to meet regularly with their staff in informal seminars. He agreed, and began holding regularly scheduled discussions about addiction. He talked about behavior therapy and the kind of patient-centered approach he was developing, and they did role-playing, with him as the care provider and them as the patients. During these sessions, the Norwegians would stop him and ask questions about what he was thinking at each step, saying things like, "You asked a question. You could ask a lot of questions. Why did you ask that one?"

It forced him to think about the way he'd talked with clients with alcohol problems since his grad school years—practices he frankly hadn't given much thought to.

When Miller was a grad student at the University of Oregon he had taken a class on how to talk about patients that was taught by a protégé of Carl Rogers, a prominent American psychologist and one of the founders of the humanistic (or client-centered) approach to psychology. The class had a distinct impact on Miller. "From the beginning it made sense to take an empathic approach" with patients, Miller said.

When Miller landed a faculty position at the University of New Mexico, he incorporated these empathic skills in with his behavioral work with patients. Before he left for Europe, he had begun conducting research on moderation training, and in his studies he had been measuring therapist empathy. The data came back just in time for him to read before he went overseas. He studied the figures and was pleasantly startled by the results, which showed that patients who'd worked with an empathetic therapist fared far better than those who had not. Patients who'd received the more compassionate counseling had shown far better rates of recovery than those who'd experienced confrontational interventions. "It had a big effect," Miller said.

Miller's hosts in Norway plied him with questions, and as he thoughtfully answered them, he began to realize that he'd discovered a potentially powerful tool in helping people overcome addiction. His answers to his interlocutors became a kind of rough draft for a practical guide to a new technique in addiction care. "It was almost the exact opposite of the in-your-face confrontation approach that was popular at the time," Miller said, referring to the intervention model developed by Hazelden. He sent his writings to some colleagues in the field, thinking them interesting but not worthy of publication. One friend who was affiliated with a journal asked if he could publish it, and Miller demurred. "I said, 'There's no data,'" Miller recalled. "But he did anyway. And it took off like a rocket."

Aside from Miller and a few of his associates, no one in the United States knew much about the method, much less used it, but the approach had gained popularity internationally. In the United Kingdom, he later learned, it had become a preferred treatment. "I had no clue this was happening," Miller said.

And Miller wouldn't learn what was happening until seven years later, when he took another sabbatical, to Australia. While there he met a psychologist named Steve Rollnick, from South Africa, who asked Miller if he was the same William Miller who'd written about motivational interviewing.

"You read it?" Miller asked, surprised.

"Read it?" Rollnick said. "I teach it."

That spurred Miller to write a book with Rollnick about the technique. It was published in 1991, and since then, the technique has taken more of a toehold in America, though it remains far from being part of standard alcoholism treatment policy. Although studies have consistently shown its efficacy, most doctors and psychologists in the United States continue to refer their patients to AA or AA-related programs.

SMART Recovery

At the same time Miller was making his discovery, others were serendipitously developing more new approaches to alcoholism recovery.

In the mid-1980s, Tom Horvath was right out of graduate school with a PhD in psychology, beginning his psychology practice and "looking for a niche," when he discovered the existence of an entire population of heavy drinkers who were willing to address their problem but were not willing to do so through the twelve-step approach of AA. "They found me," he said. "I was in general practice and several people came in with other problems, and I discovered they were drinking heavily. I told them what I knew, that they had to go to AA. They said, 'We don't want to. Can you help us?' I said, 'I don't know much.'"

With little expertise in the area, he began a personal crash course on the field, reading journal articles, stumbling onto the work of the Sobells, Miller, and others. "NIAAA had been funding research for years, and a lot of it was building up," he said.

He attended training at a program out of Southern California called New Horizons. In 1990 he found out about Rational Recovery, founded in 1985 by Jack and Lois Trimpey, social workers from Northern California. It was a recovery program based not on spiritual notions but on psychological practices that had been subjected to research. They had written a manual for their approach that they called *The Small Book*, a play on the name of AA's basic text.

Through Rational Recovery, Horvath met other psychologists who traveled similar paths. One, Tom Litwicki, a counselor and recovering alcoholic, had gained sobriety through the Twelve Steps. But when Litwicki read *The Small Book*, it opened his mind to new possibilities—though at first it frightened him. "I started questioning my own recovery—if there are other ways, maybe my way isn't so great, which means maybe my recovery is in jeopardy," he said in a later interview with historian William White. But he resolved to approach the discovery as a professional and to strive "to be compassionate and allow them to struggle with the idea that there may be more than one way to get clean and sober, and tried to roll with the resistance."

Another, Joe Gerstein, a practicing internist, had encountered patients with alcohol and drug problems, and he would later recall, "My standard practice at the time was to try to get them to go to a 12-step program of some kind," he would later say in an interview with White.

> I had all kinds of tactics and strategies of doing this, but some of them simply wouldn't go for one reason or another, wouldn't stick with it, or in some cases, attended but were not helped by it. I tried all kinds of alternatives. Some of them simply stopped using and got better on their own. One I sent to a DUI program because there was virtually nothing else. He refused to go to a psychiatrist. He loved the DUI program, and he stopped the very drastic habit, got his life back together, and his wife, who'd already given a retainer to a divorce lawyer, cancelled it. I followed him for 17 years, and he never had any problems again. So, that was in the back of my mind—people didn't have to go to a 12-step program to get better even though that was what I was taught and what I had believed.

The three started working with the Trimpeys through Rational Recovery. They developed a mutual-help component—meetings like AA but based on secular, behavioral therapy techniques, and set about trying to promote this approach to the public. "I got an article about Rational Recovery into a weekly newspaper in Boston, the *Phoenix*, and I got Jack Trimpey on a very popular talk radio program," Gerstein explained. "They kept him on for four hours. He was only supposed to be on for two hours, but the man who ran the show said, 'This is the most calls we have ever gotten on this particular radio show.' Most of them were antagonistic calls from people involved in the 12-step program, but the radio show loved the controversy."

Rational Recovery got an even bigger boost when the *Boston Globe* ran an article in the summer of 1990 about the fledgling program and Secular Organization for Sobriety, or SOS, another alternative to AA that had started in the mid-1970s. "After the *Globe* article in 1990, there were 400 calls," Gerstein recalled to White.

> I had to run home from my medical office twice to change the tape [on his answering machine]. That really was the big impetus to getting the thing going. It was a big job because everybody called on the telephone, which was in our kitchen; they wanted a meeting list and information about the program. We had to write down their name and address and then send it to them.

Later that year, the *New York Times* ran a front-page story on Rational Recovery, and its principals were invited onto the *Today* show and were given a ten-minute interview with Bryant Gumble. But just as the project was ascending, tensions arose; the Trimpeys sought to put more emphasis on their own proprietary ideas, while Horvath and Gerstein and others were gravitating more toward a science-based approach, including cognitive behavioral techniques, and motivational enhancement techniques modeled on the work of Miller. Legal disputes also arose, as the Trimpeys owned the name Rational Recovery. So there was a split within the organization in 1994, and from this rift came SMART Recovery—for Self-Management and Recovery Training.

SMART is based on a "4-point Program" of recovery: "1) building and maintaining motivation; 2) coping with urges; 3) managing thoughts, feelings, and behaviors; and 4) living a balanced life." Right away, the program began attracting members. Within a year it had ninety meetings nationwide. Said Horvath, "The SMART groups are really like seminars or workshops, where people are grappling together with ideas, not unlike the college seminars I had at St. John's College," the liberal arts college in Annapolis, Maryland, where he earned his BA.

In 1996, SMART received a $50,000 grant from the Robert Wood Johnson Foundation to train more meeting facilitators and develop a training manual, and the group continued to grow. By 2000, there were more than three hundred meetings nationwide, and today there are more than a thousand. Still, this mutual-help society's reach pales in comparison to AA, which has thousands of groups and millions of members, and Horvath fears this will ultimately doom SMART Recovery. "I'm concerned that if in the next 10 years we don't reach saturation, the program won't last," he said in an interview with the author. "We need 5,000 meetings in the U.S."

AA Defies Science

Despite the growing number of alternatives to AA and their increasing popularity, the twelve-step-centered approach continued growing in power and popularity. It not only remained the de facto treatment policy in the United States but also became downright fashionable. In the late 1980s, Michael Keaton starred in the hit movie *Clean and Sober*, and CBS aired the made-for-TV movie *My Name Is Bill W.*, about AA's cofounder Bill Wilson, starring James Woods as Wilson and James Garner as Dr. Bob. And in the early 1990s, Al Franken debuted his beloved *Saturday Night Live* character Stuart Smalley, "a member of several twelve-step programs," who hosted a public access TV show called *Daily Affirmations*. His motto: "I'm good enough, I'm smart enough, and doggone it, people like me." Franken's character not only appeared on the show numerous times throughout the 1990s but also penned a faux self-help book and played the lead in a Hollywood movie, riding a wave of recovery ephemera that flooded America. Bookstore shelves filled with hundreds of memoirs and self-help books, recovering rock stars released albums full of songs about their new sober lives, and cars everywhere bore bumper stickers with AA slogans such as "Easy Does It" and "One Day at a Time." As psychologist William White observes in *Slaying the Dragon: The History of Addiction Treatment and Recovery in America*, "Addiction recovery had gone from the shameful to the 'chic.'"

By then, Alcoholics Anonymous had more than two million members, and its Twelve Steps had been appropriated by sufferers of a host of other compulsive behaviors. There were Al-Anon, Alateen, Adult Children of Alcoholics, Co-dependents Anonymous, Narcotics Anonymous, Cocaine Anonymous, Marijuana Anonymous, Gamblers Anonymous, Debtors Anonymous, Sex Addicts Anonymous, and on and on. It seemed as though America had found in the Twelve Steps its cure for all manner of addictive and self-destructive behavior.

But did it work?

That question, scientists were finding, was very difficult to answer, despite the federal resources devoted to the problem through the NIAAA. Over the years, dozens and hundreds of papers and studies about the effectiveness of AA (or lack thereof) have been published in journals such as *Alcohol Research & Health, Journal of Addictive Diseases, The American Journal on Addictions, Journal of Studies on Alcohol and Drugs, Journal of Studies on Alcohol, Journal of Clinical Psychology, Cochrane Database of Systematic Reviews*, and *Psychology of Addictive Behaviors*, with titles like "The Evidence Base for the Effectiveness of Alcoholics Anonymous: Implications for Social Work Practice," "How Well Does AA Work? An Analysis of Published A.A. Surveys (1968–1996) and Related Analyses/Comments," "Does Alcoholics Anonymous Work? The Results from a Meta-Analysis of Controlled Experiments," "Alcoholics Anonymous Effectiveness: Faith Meets Science," and "Is Alcoholics Anonymous Effective?"

The answers are all over the map. A 2004 article in the *Journal of Counseling and Clinical Psychology*, for instance, reports the findings of a study in which the researchers recruited 628 people from a handful of detox centers, where they were referred to AA. The researchers checked up on the recruits at the one-year mark, then at three years, and then at eight. The scientists found that 70 percent of those who attended at least four meetings per week were completely sober, compared to 57 percent of those who went to between two and four per week and 21 percent of those who blew off AA completely. That's right in line with what AA claims in the Big Book: it works for three out of four who really work it. And these findings are consistent across a series of such studies. Others have shown that members of AA are more likely to stay sober if they have a sponsor and a sponsee, work the steps, lead a meeting, tell their story at a meeting, and stop hanging out with drinkers. All the stuff the old-timers tell newcomers to do.

On the other hand, there's also an earlier meta-analysis published in the journal *Substance Use & Misuse* in 1999 that found that "attending conventional AA meetings was worse than no treatment." And a series of studies that began in the mid-1990s under the direction of the late Alan Marlatt of the University of Washington have shown that if a person believes in the disease model of alcoholism provided at AA meetings he or she is more likely to eventually have a relapse into prolonged heavy drinking. This finding has been substantiated by several comprehensive follow-up studies. "Addiction treatment has suffered from perfectionism," William Miller wrote in a 2015 opinion article reflecting on what the data has shown about the AA concept of relapse and failure. "As a black-or-white dichotomy the term inherently contains what Marlatt called the 'abstinence violation effect,' that having once broken a rule all is lost."

Perhaps the most widely known statistic showing AA's ineffectiveness relative to other treatment methods is the 5 percent success rate—or 95 percent failure rate—that served as the centerpiece statistic in *The Sober Truth*, a 2014 exposé by former Harvard psychiatry professor Lance Dodes of the bad science behind AA. In fact, he gathered the statistic from AA's own surveys. Every three years since 1968 AA has randomly queried several thousands of its members for basic info—age, career, gender, how they came to AA, and length of sobriety. One of the questions AA asks is the month and year when they first came into AA. In 1990, the AA member who analyzed the results used the data to "show the probability that a member will remain in the Fellowship a given number of months." He calculated that out of every hundred people who come into AA, eighty leave within a month. At the three-month mark, only ten remain. At one year, that number has dwindled to five.

Seems straightforward: AA fails ninety-five percent of the people who come in the door.

Yet an article published in *Alcoholism Treatment Quarterly* in 2000, by Don McIntire, who lists his credentials as a "writer from Burbank," argues that the calculation is all wrong. Turns out he's a math-savvy recovering alcoholic who was sober thanks to AA for more than forty years until he died in 2007, though this affiliation isn't mentioned in the article. His argument is that the numbers are correct, but to conclude from them that AA only works for five percent of newcomers is to misunderstand how AA works. AA is not an instant cure, he explains; it takes time, effort. It works if you work it, as they say at the end of meetings, not if you go to a meeting or two and then go away. To say it fails is like saying exercise machines fail because people buy them and never use them. McIntire argues that we shouldn't count people as members until they've been around for three months. Recalculated his way, the ten who are still in AA at ninety days become a hundred and the five still standing at the end of the year become fifty. Much better.

In truth the data doesn't even tell us what McIntire claims it does. We have no idea why the survey respondents left, where they went, and what their lives were like afterward. Maybe they went straight to a bar and drank too much and died. Maybe they got everything they needed from a few meetings and went on to live soberly ever after. Maybe they weren't ready and they'll come back. Maybe they weren't even alcoholics to begin with. Maybe they're the kind of people mentioned in chapter five of the Big Book, the part they read out loud at the beginning of every AA meeting, the "people who cannot or will not completely give themselves to this simple program, usually men and women who are constitutionally incapable of being honest with themselves. There are such unfortunates. They are not at fault; they seem to have been born that way. They are naturally incapable of grasping and developing a manner of living which demands rigorous honesty."

A more detailed picture emerges from the 2006 meta-analysis by the Cochrane Collaboration of all the randomized controlled trials ever conducted to compare AA to other forms of treatment and to no treatment at all—which, as mentioned in the prologue of this book, concluded that "the available experimental studies did not demonstrate the effectiveness of AA or other 12-step approaches in reducing alcohol use." Or, more succinctly, from a 2010 editorial from *Journal of Alcohol and Drug Education*: "There are no studies that unequivocally demonstrate the effectiveness of AA."

Which is not to say science has shown AA to be ineffective, just that researchers haven't shown that it *is* effective. In other words, these studies tell us less about AA's effectiveness than they do about the difficulty of studying AA scientifically. The key issue here is the use of "randomized controlled trials" or, more accurately, the inability to do so. That's the kind of research you have to do if you want to know for sure if a medical treatment works. It's how scientists test drugs—they take a group of volunteers and give half of them the drug they want to study and give the other half a different drug or a placebo, and then they record the effects and compare results. This is hard to do with AA. Some say it's impossible, because the way AA works for most people is they hit bottom and then go to AA for help. It's a choice. If you take the choice away, you're not really studying how it works. (In fact, one of the few things science has shown with some certainty is that if you force people to go to AA, as a punishment for a crime, for example, or through a Dr. Drew Pinsky–style intervention, it tends to make their alcoholism worse.) There are ethical concerns, too. If you have a group of subjects who are alcoholics in need of help, is it right to randomly assign them to no treatment when it's possible AA could save their lives? Or the other way around: if it's true AA makes the problem worse, is it ethical to send them to a meeting? Then there's the nature of AA itself. It's an anonymous program controlled entirely from the bottom up. An anarchy, in essence. It defies science, defies it so thoroughly that just about every article to be found on the subject contains a passage lamenting the lack of scientific evidence about it.

A Little Yellow Pill

In 1995, newspapers across the country ran a curious wire story about a woman named Margaret Catrambone of Clifton Heights, Pennsylvania, who claimed to have been cured of her alcoholism with a pill. The story said she had struggled with her drinking problem for fifteen years, had tried AA and counseling with no luck. "They might work for a week but then I'd be back on the bottle," the article quoted her as saying. "Just one drink would tip me back over the edge. I would just pick up the bottle and drink until it was gone."

But then her doctor told her about a clinical trial at the University of Pennsylvania of a drug thought to help alcoholics quit or cut back on drinking. The tests were being conducted by Dr. Joseph Volpicelli, director of the university's treatment research center, who administered daily doses of a drug called naltrexone and provided weekly counseling sessions.

"I was a wreck," Catrambone recalled of her earliest days in the experiment. "On the first day I cried for two hours. I had a counselor on one side of me, and the doctor's assistant on the other. I had to take one tablet a day, and I suffered terrible cravings, but I forced myself to take things one day at a time."

Four months later, she claimed she was cured. "By the time I'd finished the course of treatment and come off the tablets, the craving was gone," she told reporters. "And without that, I just didn't have the desire to drink."

Enoch Gordis, director of the NIAAA at the time, declared in the article, "This is the beginning of a new era in alcoholism treatment." But others quoted in the article—practitioners in the treatment industry—were unconvinced. "I don't see this as anything our doctors would prescribe," said Dolores Hughes, director of privately run addiction treatment facilities on Long Island. "It seems alcoholics look for a quick fix and it doesn't work. And taking a pill is a quick fix."

Laura Mastrangelo, spokeswoman for DuPont Merck, the drug's manufacturer, said, "We're not going to convince everyone, and it's not going to be used by everyone. We understand there's going to be resistance. Over time, we're convinced there will be enough studies to show what the success rate will be."

Naltrexone was originally synthesized in 1963 by Endo Laboratories, a small pharmaceutical company in Long Island, New York, and patented in 1967. In 1969, DuPont purchased Endo Laboratories, and at the time the company didn't show as much interest in naltrexone as it did in other drugs developed by Endo. But in March 1972, Congress passed the Drug Abuse Office and Treatment Act, which carried a provision to encourage development of "long-lasting, non-addictive, blocking and antagonist drugs or other pharmacological substances for the treatment of heroin addiction" as a means of addressing the problem of soldiers coming back from Vietnam with heroin habits. Naltrexone had shown some potential for inhibiting the effects of heroin, thereby reducing the user's desire for the drug. The trials of naltrexone lasted twelve years, and the results were disappointing—the scientists found it was difficult to get addicts to follow the treatment regimen, which commenced with a monthlong period of abstinence.

Meanwhile, Volpicelli at Penn discovered through experiments with rats that the drug had the potential to reduce cravings for alcohol and began publishing his findings in the early 1980s. In 1985, he embarked on a study using alcoholic volunteers from a VA hospital. "We did it without any outside funding," Dr. Charles O'Brien, a professor at Penn and chief of psychiatry at Philadelphia's Veterans Administration Medical Center, told researchers in a later interview. "We got it started against pretty great odds."

The odds against them grew greater because researchers had a hard time recruiting subjects—treatment counselors refused to make referrals. The notion of using drugs to treat alcoholics was seen as sacrilegious in that community. Volpicelli and his team managed to amass just seventy subjects, all male, for a three-month outpatient program, giving half of them naltrexone, the other half a placebo. Only one in four of those on naltrexone relapsed into alcoholic drinking, while more than half of those taking a placebo did.

In 1991, researchers at the Yale School of Medicine conducted another study with the drug, funded by the NIAAA. They administered naltrexone and provided psychological therapy to more than one hundred severe alcoholics, both male and female, and this yielded a similarly high success rate. "Until recently, we had relied heavily on psychological prevention," said Stephanie O'Malley, the Yale researcher who authored the study. "The good news in our study is that the majority of patients who received naltrexone and therapy were doing well after six months."

But like their colleagues in Pennsylvania, the Yale scientists had trouble finding subjects, so they accepted every volunteer they could get. This likely skewed the results, because the subjects were invariably the hardest cases and it was probable that the medicine would be more effective for less severely afflicted problem drinkers. It also meant they had issues with patient compliance. Dropout rates were high.

Still, the results were strong enough to spur the FDA to approve naltrexone in fifty-milligram doses for the treatment of alcoholism in 1995. Holding a patent for the drug, which the government had extended to encourage its development as a cure for alcoholism, DuPont marketed it under the brand name ReVia. The approval came with foreboding caveats, however—warning labels stressed that the drug should be prescribed only along with a rigorous regimen of counseling and therapy. "ReVia should be considered as only one of many factors determining the success of treatment of alcoholism," the labels read. This proved enough to discourage doctors from offering the drug to their patients.

Another impediment to its adoption as a common remedy was DuPont's choice to market it to treatment centers, which were steeped in AA dogma and preternaturally opposed to the use of drugs in treatment. Their aim was for a spiritual transformation, not a chemical one. Reid Hester recalled being approached by the company to serve as a spokesman. "They said they were going to target treatment providers," he said. "I said, 'You're barking up the wrong tree.' They spent millions to target treatment providers and got nowhere."

Hester told them they should market to family doctors. But according to a 1996 report on the drug cited by the US Department of Health and Human Services, "While DuPont could have marketed its product directly to general practitioners, there were many reasons why it did not. DuPont did not want naltrexone to be falsely construed as a 'miracle pill' that would 'cure alcoholism,' because it could not stop all alcoholics from drinking, especially without counseling from comprehensive treatment centers."

Insurance companies also balked at covering it. So sales of naltrexone fell far short of DuPont's projections, which were modest to begin with. In interviews with market analysts conducting a study of the drug's failure, DuPont executives had said they'd taken the drug on as a public service. But when the patent expired in the late 1990s, the company no longer had any incentive to promote the drug, so it sat on pharmacy shelves with FDA approval but few doctors who even knew about it, much less had the willingness to prescribe it. And so untold numbers of alcoholics who might have benefitted from naltrexone went on struggling with their problems, unaware that a simple yellow pill was out there as an option.

A Final Blow Against Controlled Drinking

Throughout her early twenties, Audrey Kishline, a Michigan homemaker, drank to drunkenness nearly every day, alone or with friends, and she woke up most mornings with a hideous hangover. Worst of all, she'd sometimes get behind the wheel when she was tipsy or even seeing double. As she neared her thirtieth birthday, her life got worse and worse. Twice she checked into treatment programs, she visited countless therapists and doctors, and she attended AA meetings. But nothing stuck.

"I just felt that I didn't really fit that model," she told the *New York Times* in 1995, referring to the kind of alcoholic described in AA's Big Book. She was still functioning at a fairly high level, managing her home, caring for her children, and, when she needed to, she could control her consumption of booze. "I had a lot of problems with the powerlessness and the disease issue and the label of alcoholism," she said.

The best she could manage after undergoing this treatment was to go from being a daily drinker to a binge drinker—she'd be abstinent for days and weeks, sometimes months on end, then succumb to her cravings and have a drink and then keep drinking until she was obliterated. The concept of alcoholism as a disease was for her like a self-fulfilling prophesy. "In my opinion, my ability to change my drinking behavior was delayed considerably because of traditional treatment," she later told another newspaper reporter. "I went on a huge detour," adding: "If I had been properly assessed as a problem, rather than a chronic, drinker and offered the option of moderation as a self-management goal, I never would have experienced such years of emotional pain."

She started doing research into alcoholism to see if there were any alternatives to AA and total abstinence, and she found studies showing that moderation and controlled drinking worked for some problem drinkers. She decided to give it a try. It seemed to work, so she wrote a book about her discovery, called *Moderate Drinking: The New Option for Problem Drinkers*, published by See Sharp Press, and founded the Moderation Management Network, a mutual-help organization modeled after AA, with regular meetings and a multistep course of action. MM's nine-step approach starts with a thirty-day period of abstinence during which members examine how drinking has affected their lives, assess "how much, how often and under what circumstances" they drink, and write down life priorities before setting weekly moderation guidelines. Going forward, members regularly assess their progress.

MM's guidelines for moderate drinking are based on NIAAA standards— for women a maximum of three drinks a day, nine drinks a week; men no more than four drinks a day, fourteen per week. MM calls for three abstinence days every week.

If members can't manage to keep their drinking down to these levels, they're encouraged to quit altogether. "The goal of this whole thing is to reduce your drinking to a level that no longer causes problems," Kishline told the Philadelphia *Inquirer*. "That may be moderation, or that may be total abstinence." The vast majority of adults who have a "drinking problem" aren't alcoholics, she added. "Those are the people we can help at very early stages."

Her book, the new mutual support society, and a smattering of news reports about her efforts from papers around the country generated significant interest. She received hundreds of letters every week, and new MM groups popped up across the country. Other moderation programs came online as well. In the mid-1990s, the Center of Alcohol Studies, a research institute at Rutgers University in Piscataway, New Jersey, established a treatment program to help alcohol abusers reduce their drinking through short-term counseling sessions known as brief interventions. The Rutgers center catered to people with drinking problems that fall short of the full-blown addicted level Jellinek called "gamma" in his book on the disease concept of alcoholism. They were people for whom alcohol had caused a significant problem but who could, when necessary, exert a modicum of control over their consumption. The scientists at Rutgers would assess whether or not potential patients were viable candidates for the treatment by administering neurological and blood tests and asking a long list of detailed questions about drinking behavior.

Another moderation initiative developed around this time was Drink-Wise, an alcohol management program established in 1994 at the University of Michigan Medical Center in Ann Arbor that helps people moderate their drinking through short-term group or one-on-one counseling. "There's more than one type of drinker, and there needs to be more than one type of treatment program," explained DrinkWise's project manager Keith D. Bruhnsen.

Still, some longstanding alcohol treatment centers, while providing an array of treatment options from low-intensity outpatient counseling to monthlong inpatient treatment, continued to stand by the abstinence model and involvement in AA, and many of its practitioners were outspoken in their opposition to using moderation as an option in any case. It would be safer, they argued, to treat all problem drinkers the same and urge them to quit drinking entirely. "In general, it's not a good idea under any circumstances to encourage an alcoholic to moderate, or the heavy drinker whose natural history would be to go on to alcoholism," said Dr. Daniel K. Flavin, director of the National Council on Alcoholism and Drug Dependence, formerly the NCA, Marty Mann's organization. "How do you tease those people out?"

Similarly, Gerald Horowitz, the administrator of the Smithers Alcoholism Treatment and Training Center at St. Luke's–Roosevelt Hospital Center in Manhattan, frowns on prescribing different treatments for patients with less-severe drinking problems. "We don't necessarily see problem drinkers and alcoholics as different," he told the *New York Times* in 2015. "We see them as two different stages of the same disease. People who are real concerned about their alcohol or drug consumption are concerned for a reason."

"It's like driving your car without a spare tire," observed Dr. George E. Vaillant, a psychiatry professor at Harvard Medical School and author of *The Natural History of Alcoholism Revisited.* "You can do it for a while. The people who go back to social drinking tend to be borderline."

Dr. Frederick Rotgers, an assistant research professor and director of research protocols at the Rutgers center, said: "Unfortunately, in this country, for many, many years even to talk about people with a drinking problem simply cutting down has been anathema. Among dyed-in-the-wool 12-step followers, it is heresy. Among pragmatic people who are reading the scientific literature, it's no longer heresy."

Still, Kishline was optimistic that moderation would take hold in the American treatment industrial complex, telling a Saint Paul *Pioneer Press* reporter, "I predict within five to 10 years every treatment center soon will offer a treatment for moderation." And when the Smithers treatment center instituted, despite Horowitz's admonition, a controlled-drinking option for patients who shunned AA and abstinence, it appeared as though her prediction would come to fruition.

But at the same time, Kishline was hiding a secret. She'd been drinking immoderately, even as she was trumpeting her MM. Finally, her drinking got so bad that she wrote an open letter to members of MM and announced she was going back to AA. Still, she drank uncontrollably. Then one night she drove the wrong way down a four-lane highway, dead drunk, and killed a man and his twelve-year-old daughter. She had a blood-alcohol level more than three times the legal limit and was convicted of vehicular homicide, serving four years in jail.

Critics of moderation were quick to pounce on the tragedy as proof that abstinence is the only solution. Marty Mann's organization, now named the National Council on Alcoholism and Drug Dependence, said the tragedy taught a "harsh lesson for all of society, particularly those individuals who collude with the media to continually question abstinence-based treatment for problems related to alcohol and other drugs." And after the crash, Kishline, through her attorney, condemned her own creation, Moderation Management, as "nothing but alcoholics covering up their problem."

The accident drew national news coverage, including a long report on ABC's *20/20* about moderation as a recovery option. Among those featured in the episode was Dr. Alexander DeLuca, medical director for the Smithers treatment center in Manhattan, who explained why the famed center, established by and named after R. Brinkley Smithers, the longtime benefactor of Marty Mann's campaign to sell the nation on the disease model of alcoholism, now offered controlled-drinking training as an option.

"We do find that people who go to twelve-step meetings do better," he said to the *20/20* cameras, referring to the recovery model pioneered by AA. "But it doesn't work for some and I'm not going to tell them, 'Come back after you've suffered some more and are ready to do it our way.'" He went on to say, "The system we have fails to engage the majority. The system we have tends to push people away, to become potentially sicker. The system we have does a poor job of engaging people early on the continuum of illness as is standard medical practice for any of the other 'chronic, relapsing diseases.'"

In exchange for his honesty and adherence to scientific principles, DeLuca not only lost his job, but his reputation was destroyed. The Smithers Foundation immediately called for his resignation and took out a full-page ad in the *New York Times* chastising the doctor and his colleagues for not having "learned their ABCs: A=Alcoholism is a disease; B=Booze has no place in its treatment; C=Controlled Drinking does not work." The foundation's president sent out a letter saying that this move to include moderation training among its treatment options "will most certainly spawn new moderation management treatment models around the country. Alcoholics will be enticed to go into treatment without having to give up drinking! The tragedy is that lives will be destroyed and people will die in the process."

EPILOGUE

2000–PRESENT:
STUCK IN THE 1950S

HIDDEN IN THE DEEP recesses of the National Institutes of Health's sprawling campus in Bethesda, Maryland, at the end of a long hospital corridor, behind a locked door, is a fully stocked and functioning bar and lounge. It's a small, narrow space, no bigger than a dorm room. Posters advertising beer, wine, and hard liquor are hung on the walls, and at one end of the room is a small wood-topped bar, with shelves full of hard liquor bottles and a sign that reads, "The Bar is Open." There's a sink and four beer taps—Sierra Nevada, Heineken, Bass, Budweiser—and a flat-screen TV. Its seating area is cramped, with just a couple of small round tables and simple chairs.

Dr. Lorenzo Leggio, an NIAAA scientist and a native of Italy, switched off the overhead fluorescent lights and dialed up dim lamp lights, giving the room an ambience suitable for drinking. "How it usually works when we have an experimental session," he said, "our physician, he's sitting here on the sofa, and one of our students will act as a bartender, and the subject will drink water first, as a control cue, and then alcohol. It's personalized, so if people like Budweiser, they will actually have Budweiser. If they drink a type of wine, merlot, they will have merlot. They even see the name."

Leggio is chief of the NIAAA's Section on Clinical Psychoneuroendocrinology and Neuropsychopharmacology, which seeks medicines that will help people with drinking problems drink less or stop completely. The bar is part of his lab, and its purpose is to help better understand how problem drinkers respond to the first drink. In a corner stands a medical monitoring machine, the kind a nurse might hook up to a patient to read blood pressure during a routine checkup. During experiments, his team of scientists checks blood pressure and heart rate at regular intervals between drinks and measures salivation by placing dental cotton balls between the subjects' cheeks and gums and weighing them on a digital scale before and after. "We know that people have a higher craving for alcohol, they also have higher salivation, higher heart rate, and higher blood pressure," he explained. "So we measure all these in real time. We find that when people have lower craving, they also have lower salivation, lower blood pressure, lower heart rate."

Leggio and his team use the bar/lab to explore what he calls "gut/liver/brain axis," an internal system in which abdominal hormones "communicate" with the mind and, studies have shown, affect the level of craving alcoholics have for alcohol. Chief among these hormones is ghrelin, a naturally occurring compound, that was discovered only in 1999. "Ghrelin is a hormone which is produced by the stomach," said Leggio. "We all have ghrelin in our body. And what happens is, when I'm starving, one of the reasons I'm starving is because my ghrelin levels are very high. So the stomach is now releasing a lot of ghrelin in the body, and the ghrelin is communicating to my brain. This hormone travels from the stomach up to the brain and is able to cross what we call blood-brain barrier and it goes into receptors in the brain, so it's telling to my brain, 'Lorenzo, you are better off to eat now.'"

In the early 2000s, scientists experimenting on mice found that when they gave the rodents ghrelin, it would increase their desire for alcohol. "So we took a population of alcoholic people and we studied their ghrelin levels," Leggio said. "And we saw that the factor was consistent with the animal data because we saw that people with lower ghrelin levels had lower cravings for alcohol and they were more likely to maintain abstinence. So we gave ghrelin intravenously and we controlled with placebo and we tested craving in a bar laboratory setting, in real time—testing how much people crave alcohol after this pharmacological challenge. And we found that in fact after receiving ghrelin, these patients had much higher cravings in alcohol."

Leggio's bar/lab existence is a testament to how much the institute has evolved since its inception in the early 1970s, when Marty Mann and other powerful AA activists held sway. Back then, such experimentation with controlled drinking would have been scandalous. Now it's central to the institute's mission and more in line with what the scientists at the American Association for the Advancement of Science had in mind when they formed a council on alcohol in the late 1930s. It represents an absolute victory over those who sought in the institute's early days to make it a federal wing of Alcoholics Anonymous, spreading the word about alcoholism as a disease and AA as its cure. The research has revealed new possibilities for treatment recovery and also established a national norm for not drinking during pregnancy, as part of a public information campaign.

The section Leggio heads is part of the NIAAA's intramural research program, which seeks, according to its mission statement, to "unravel the biological basis for alcohol use disorders and related problems and to develop new strategies for treatment and prevention." It consists of thirteen labs focused on areas such as cardiovascular physiology and neurogenic molecular physiology. The institute also supports a network of extramural research centers at top universities across the country, such as Brown University, the University of New Mexico, and Case Western Reserve University, through hundreds of millions of dollars worth of research grants.

After touring Leggio's lab, I met with Dr. George Koob, director of the NIAAA. His background is in neurobiology, and he told me that the research of Leggio and other scientists in the NIAAA's programs holds "the future of recovery in America." In addition to ghrelin suppressants, the NIAAA has other drugs in the pipeline that that also show a lot of promise, Koob said. "My plan is to shift more resources toward medication development," he told me. "It is a high priority," he said, adding: "We've hit a turning point with treatment of addictions and alcohol use disorders where we really have embraced the concept that addiction and alcoholism are brain diseases. This will lead to them being treated more like diabetes, with medicine. My plan is to shift more resources toward medication development. It's a high priority."

It's a laudable goal, one that resonates with me personally. It was a medicine—naltrexone—that helped me turn a corner on my own drinking problem and to forge my own path to recovery. After almost thirty years of believing my only choice was to go to AA or drink myself to death, I read an article about the drug and found a doctor who prescribed it to me. It didn't completely eliminate my craving for alcohol, but when I drank after taking one of the little yellow pills, I found that my compulsion to binge drink lessened. When I would drink, I drank less than usual, and the days when I did drink gradually became fewer and fewer. Feeling better, I looked for more tools to help me reduce the harm I was inflicting on myself with repeated heavy drinking. I started participating in SMART Recovery meetings online, and I downloaded a cognitive behavioral therapy app called CheckUp & Choices, which allowed me to track my cravings for alcohol and to aid me in my decisions around alcohol, to decide on my own accord, for instance, to go for a run or read a book or do anything other than drink alcoholically. I'm not 100 percent abstinent, but my lapses into excessive drinking are short-lived and fewer and further between. Most days, I find that the easiest course of action is to abstain completely, but I also know that if I have a drink or two at an office function or at a fancy dinner with my wife, it doesn't mean that I have to keep pounding drinks until I pass out.

Science shows us, in overwhelming and unambiguous data, that this is how the vast majority of people with drinking problems recover: outside of AA, often with no treatment at all. And a great many go on to drink like normal people, in moderation. In America there are twenty-five to forty million people who have recovered from alcoholism and addiction, and fewer than 20 percent of them did it by quitting completely, still fewer as lifelong members of AA. In the words of the federally funded researcher who calculated those figures (from more than four hundred studies dating back to 1868): "Insanity, prolonged institutionalization, and death are not the normative outcomes of alcoholism and addiction. Recovery is not an aberration achieved by a small and morally enlightened minority of addicted people. If there is a natural developmental momentum within the course of alcoholism and addiction, it is toward remission and recovery."

Dr. William White, who completed the above-referenced study, has said,

> The disease concept that emerged in the mid-20th century was a beautiful concept for its time. It "worked" in the truest sense and it worked at personal, professional and cultural levels. However, this concept enters the 21st century with: 1) a poor scientific foundation; 2) a narrowly defined clinical profile that does not reflect the diversity of individuals seeking help for alcohol- and other drug-related problems; and 3) a poorly defined boundary that leaves it open to continued corruption and commercial exploitation.

Yet the story of the disease concept of alcoholism that Marty Mann and her nationwide network of AA members told and retold throughout the latter half of the twentieth century remains the dominant narrative in the field. It's so dominant that it takes great effort to even find out about, much less locate, alternatives to AA. For example, I had great difficulty finding a doctor who would prescribe naltrexone to me. Although the NIAAA has been declaring for the last twenty years in its published materials that we are now at a point with medications and other forms of treatment that alcohol problems can be addressed by family doctors, much the way depression and anxiety are now dealt with, it's difficult to find doctors who will prescribe these remedies. Most physicians continue the practice, developed many decades ago, of referring alcoholics to specialists, the overwhelming majority of whom subscribe to the AA-based abstinence model. It was the same with my doctor. I had to contact several psychiatrists in my area before I could find one who would prescribe naltrexone to me.

The result of this is that most people with drinking problems don't seek help at all. The results from a national epidemiological survey on alcohol problems published in 2007 in the *Archives of General Psychiatry* (now called *JAMA Psychiatry*) revealed that less than a quarter of all Americans who struggle with drinking problems seek or receive any help at all. And a report published six years later in *JAMA: The Journal of the American Medical Association*, found that fewer than one in ten are prescribed medicine such as naltrexone or acamprosate to help them quit or reduce their drinking, despite the fact that both drugs had been approved for such usage for nearly twenty years.

In an accompanying editorial, the journal decried that alcoholics "receive poorer-quality care than patients with any other common chronic condition" and urged care providers to begin using these medicines to help their patients.

The report received a fair amount of press coverage. In the *New York Times*, the paper's lead author, Dr. Daniel E. Jonas, an associate professor of medicine at the University of North Carolina, said, "These drugs are really underused quite a bit, and our findings show that they can help thousands and thousands of people. They're not blockbuster. They're not going to work for everybody. But they can make a difference for a lot of people."

The problem, Jonas explained to NPR, is that doctors simply don't know about the medications. "It's been quite a bit of a secret," he said. "It doesn't get advertised."

Koob said at the time of the report's release that he hoped it would persuade more doctors to consider using the drugs, telling the *Times*, "This is an important paper. There are effective medications for the treatment of alcoholism, and it would be great if the world would use them."

"I don't think much has changed at this point," he said to me about the report. "The data still indicate that only about 20 percent of individuals with an alcohol use disorder get any treatment at all, and only 10 percent get any pharmaceutical treatment."

But when I met with Koob in his office and asked what is the biggest challenge he and the NIAAA face, he didn't say anything about educating the public about what we now understand about alcoholism and its treatment. "Lack of funds" is the biggest challenge, he said. "I don't think anybody at NIH is going to say anything else. The budget's been flat for ten years, and that means our buying power has been declining. And we have just this wonderful cadre of young people interested in the field, interested in solving some of these medical problems, and they're and we're in danger of losing a generation of young people, scientists, and researchers."

I interviewed Koob in early 2016, and since then the situation has gotten worse. At the time, the institute's budget had been a little more than $400 million for the previous ten years. When a new administration came into power after the 2016 election, however, it moved to slash the institute's budget, along with scores of other domestic programs. The proposed cut was steep indeed—$100 million, a quarter of the NIAAA's budget. As a result, the institute has sought additional forms of funding, including from the liquor industry. In 2014, the institute quietly solicited contributions from liquor companies to fund a study of whether or not moderate, daily drinking is beneficial to heart health, as has been widely reported but with scant research to support it. The *New York Times* exposed the gambit in early 2016, a congressional backlash ensued, the study was canceled, and the funds were returned. Koob also took heat for shifting money away from studies of the effects of alcohol advertising on teens—reportedly telling the scientists behind the study, "I don't fucking care!"—to conduct research along the lines of Leggio's.

But from my perspective, after spending several years researching the history of alcoholism and its treatment in the United States, and after my own difficult process of even so much as learning the existence of alternatives to AA, what the institute and the field of alcoholism treatment need is another Marty Mann, one who sells the nation not on alcoholism as a disease in her own image but to help us understand alcohol use disorders as they actually are.

To this end, I asked Koob to what extent the NIAAA works with the NCADD, what the organization Mann created, still in operation, is now called.

Koob stared back at me blankly.

"The National Council on Alcoholism and Drug Dependence," I said, spelling out for him the name of the organization most responsible for the very institute he was then the head of.

"I don't know that organization," he admitted. "I've only been on this job for two years, but I've never heard of that."

"It's the organization whose campaign basically created the institute you now head," I said, trying to suppress my incredulity.

He shrugged, groaned, and turned to his public information officer, who was sitting in on the interview. "We'll look at that," the PIO said. "If Ken's around, we can ask him, because I don't know the answer to that," referring to Ken Warren, one of the few officials still remaining at the NIAAA who had been there when Mann and the pro-AA contingency wielded heavy influence over the institute.

"I'm guessing that we will be happy to provide them with [the] evidence-based information that we have," Koob offered. "But I don't know of any formal relationship."

I gave a quick summary of the history of the alcoholism movement. Some of it rang a bell with him, reminding him of a documentary he'd seen about the emergence of alcohol and drug addiction treatment programs in the United States, called *Anonymous People*.

"We have websites," he said. "The website we have is rethinkingdrinking.com. [The actual URL is www.rethinkingdrinking.niaaa.nih.gov.] Go on there. You can look at your favorite drink; if it's a mixed drink, you can calculate how much alcohol is in it. You can look up what constitutes a drink. You can look at what causes a blackout. You can find out how many calories in a drink. You can find a lot of information if you just Google rethinkingdrinking.com. You'll find the website."

ACKNOWLEDGMENTS

THIS BOOK WAS MADE POSSIBLE in part by a University Grant from Columbus State University, a Moody Research Grant from the LBJ Foundation, and a Loudermilk Grant from the CSU department of English.

I wish to thank my literary agent, Ayesha Pande, for staying with me through the years it took to develop this book, and for finding a home for it. Thank you as well to Yuval Taylor, Devon Freeny, and the entire staff at Chicago Review Press, for their belief in the project and their expert guidance.

I'm grateful to the Syracuse University Libraries, the Brown University Archives, the LBJ Presidential Library, and the National Archives in College Park, Maryland, for their holdings and their attentive and helpful staffs. I'm also thankful to the many people who took time from their busy lives to grant interviews, including Amy Bach, Joseph Califano Jr., Elliott Hagan Jr., Reid Hester, Tom Horvath, Peter Hutt, George Koob, Lorenzo Leggio, William Miller, Mark and Linda Sobell, Marsha Vannicelli, and Kenneth Warren.

This book would not have been possible were it not for the scholarship that proceeded it. I am especially indebted to the PhD dissertations of Ron Roizen, Bruce Holley Johnson, and Robin Room, as well as William White's *Slaying the Dragon: The History of Addiction Treatment and Recovery in America* and his voluminous online repository, the William White Papers (www.william whitepapers.com).

And I am deeply indebted to my friends and family who supported me through this long and sometimes difficult project, especially Gary Sprayberry, who read the manuscript prior to submission, and my wife, Allie Johnson, who read many drafts along the way and, unlike me, never once doubted the project.

BIBLIOGRAPHY

A.A. Grapevine. "The Little Doctor Who Loved Drunks." May 1951.

Abraham, Amanda J., Traci Rieckmann, Thomas Mcnulty, Anne E. Kovas, and Paul M. Roman. "Counselor Attitudes Toward the Use of Naltrexone in Substance Abuse Treatment: A Multi-level Modeling Approach." *Addictive Behaviors* 36, no. 6 (2011).

Addiction. "Conversation with Senator Harold Hughes." Vol. 92, no. 2 (1997).

Alcohol Health & Research World. "Reflections: NIAAA's Directors Look Back on 25 Years." Vol. 19, no. 1 (1995).

Alcoholics Anonymous. *Alcoholics Anonymous.* New York: Alcoholics Anonymous World Services, 1938.

———. *Dr. Bob and the Good Oldtimers: A Biography, with Recollections of Early AA in the Midwest.* New York: Alcoholics Anonymous World Services, 1980.

———. *"Pass It On": The Story of Bill Wilson and How the A.A. Message Reached the World.* New York: Alcoholics Anonymous World Services, 1984.

———. *Twelve Steps and Twelve Traditions.* New York: Alcoholics Anonymous World Services, 1952.

Alcoholism & Drug Abuse Weekly. "Targeted Naltrexone: Taking a Pill and Intending to Drink—but Less." March 30, 2009.

Aldhous, Peter. "Prescription: Sobriety." *New Scientist,* January 9, 2010.

Alexander, Jack. "Alcoholics Anonymous." *Saturday Evening Post,* March 1, 1941.

Anderson, Dwight. "Alcohol and Public Opinion." *Quarterly Journal of Studies on Alcohol* 3, no. 3 (December 1942).

Anderson, Jon. "A Sobering View of Drinking." *Chicago Tribune,* January 6, 1987.

Armor, David J., J. Michael Polich, and Harriet B. Stambul. *Alcoholism Treatment.* Santa Monica: Rand Corporation, 1976.

ASAM News. "New Definition for Alcoholism." March/April 1990.

Associated Press. "Alcoholics-Group Founder in Death Crash." *Vancouver Province,* June 28, 2000.

————. "Researcher Repudiates Study on Alcoholic Social Drinking." *New York Times*, August 26, 1982.

B., Dick. *That Amazing Grace: The Role of Clarence and Grace S. in Alcoholics Anonymous*. San Rafael, CA: Paradise Research Publications, 1996.

Bach, Amy. Telephone interview by author, February 16, 2016.

Barefoot's World. "Charles B. Towns, Ph.D." 2009. www.barefootsworld.org/aacharles _towns.html.

Bebbington, Paul E. "The Efficacy of Alcoholics Anonymous: The Elusiveness of the Hard Data." *British Journal of Psychiatry* 128, no. 6 (1976).

Block, Marvin A. "Alcohol, Man and Science." Speech to the 12th Annual Texas Summer Studies on Alcohol, University of Texas, Austin, TX, July 13, 1969.

————. "Comment on Davies DL: Normal Drinking in Recovered Alcohol Addicts." *Quarterly Journal of Studies on Alcohol* 24 (1963).

————. "Prevention of Alcoholism: To Eliminate the Disease." Speech at the University of Nevada, Reno, NV, July 27, 1972.

Boffey, Philip M. "Controlled Drinking Gains as a Treatment in Europe." *New York Times*, November 22, 1983.

————. "Panel Clears 2 Accused of Scientific Fraud in Alcoholism Study." *New York Times*, November 5, 1982.

————. "Panel Finds No Fraud by Alcohol Researchers." *New York Times*, September 11, 1984.

————. "Showdown Nears in Feud over Alcohol Studies." *New York Times*, November 2, 1982.

Bor, Jonathan. "Drug for Alcoholism Wins Praise Tempered with Skepticism." *Baltimore Sun*, January 22, 1995.

Bowman, Karl M., and E. M. Jellinek. "Alcohol Addiction and Its Treatment." *Journal of Studies on Alcohol* 2 (September 1941).

Bradley, Katherine A. "The Primary Care Practitioner's Role in the Prevention and Management of Alcohol Problems." *Alcohol Research & Health* 18, no. 2 (1994).

Bradley, Katharine A., and Daniel R. Kivlahan. "Bringing Patient-Centered Care to Patients with Alcohol Use Disorders." *JAMA* 311, no. 18 (May 14, 2014).

British Journal of Addiction. "Conversation with D. L. Davies." Vol. 74, no. 3 (September 1979).

Brown, David R. *A Biography of Mrs. Marty Mann: The First Lady of Alcoholics Anonymous*. Center City, MN: Hazelden, 2005.

Buenker, John D. "Hughes, Harold Everett." *The Biographical Dictionary of Iowa*. Iowa City: University of Iowa Press, 2009.

Burger, Margaret R. Letter to Marty Mann, December 12, 1944. Syracuse University Libraries.

Cain, Arthur H. "Alcoholics Anonymous: Cult or Cure?" *Harper's*, February 1963.

———. "Alcoholics Can Be Cured—Despite A.A." *Saturday Evening Post*, September 19, 1964.

———. *The Cured Alcoholic: New Concepts in Alcoholism Treatment and Research.* New York: John Day, 1964.

Califano, Joseph A., Jr. Remarks to the National Council on Alcoholism, Sheraton Park Hotel, Washington, DC, May 1, 1979.

———. Telephone interview by author, November 27, 2017.

Carpenter, Thomas P. Letter to President Lyndon B. Johnson, April 7, 1967. LBJ Presidential Library.

Cater, Douglass. Letter to Marty Mann, April 1, 1966. LBJ Presidential Library.

———. Memo to secretary of health, education, and welfare, June 9, 1966. LBJ Presidential Library.

Chafetz, Morris E., and Harold W. Demone. *Alcoholism and Society.* Oxford: Oxford University Press, 1970.

Charles B. Towns Hospital. *The Work of the Charles B. Towns Hospital and Its Relation to the Medical Profession.* New York: Charles B. Towns Hospital, 1918.

Cheever, Susan. *My Name Is Bill: Bill Wilson—His Life and the Creation of Alcoholics Anonymous.* New York: Washington Square, 2005.

Christian Century. "Alcohol Control Must Be Studied." October 12, 1938.

Clark, Juliette W. Letter to E. H. Curtis, January 16, 1963. Syracuse University Libraries.

———. Letter to E. L. Derby, January 28, 1963. Syracuse University Libraries.

———. Letter to Andrew Jensen, May 21, 1963. Syracuse University Libraries.

———. Letter to Mrs. Donald C. Pricer, April 9, 1963. Syracuse University Libraries.

Collins, Frederick L. "Prohibition—Will It Happen Again?" *Liberty*, June 27, 1942.

Connors, G. J., J. S. Tonigan, and W. R. Miller. "A Longitudinal Model of Intake Symptomatology, AA Participation and Outcome: Retrospective Study of the Project MATCH Outpatient and Aftercare Samples." *Journal of Studies on Alcohol* 62, no. 6 (November 2001).

Cunningham, John A. "The Use of Emerging Technologies in Alcohol Treatment." *Alcohol Research & Health* 33, no. 4 (2011).

Curtis, E. H. Letter to Marty Mann, January 18, 1963. Syracuse University Libraries.

Dabney, Virginius. "The Ghost Has Not Gone Wet." *Ken*, August 25, 1938.

Davies, D. L. "Normal Drinking in Recovered Alcohol Addicts." *Quarterly Journal of Studies on Alcohol* 23 (March 1962).

Davis, Elrick B. "Alcoholics Anonymous Makes Its Stand Here." *Cleveland Plain Dealer*, October–November 1939. Via Silkworth.net, http://silkworth.net/pages/ebd/index.php.

Delbanco, Andrew, and Thomas Delbanco. "A.A. at the Crossroads." *New Yorker*, March 20, 1995.

Dodes, Lance M., and Zachary Dodes. *The Sober Truth: Debunking the Bad Science Behind 12-Step Programs and the Rehab Industry*. Boston: Beacon Press, 2015.

Drug and Alcohol Review. "Personal Perspectives: An Interview with Mark and Linda Sobell." Vol. 10, no. 4 (1991).

Easter v. District of Columbia. US Court of Appeals, District of Columbia Circuit, March 31, 1966.

Ellison, Jerome. "Alcoholics Anonymous—Dangers of Success." *Nation*, March 2, 1964.

Emrick, Chad D. "Alcoholics Anonymous: Affiliation Processes and Effectiveness as Treatment." *Alcoholism: Clinical and Experimental Research* 12, no. 1 (February 1987).

Feder, Philip. "Trustee Pike Discusses Alcoholic Past." *Stanford Daily*, May 25, 1976.

Felix, Robert H. "Remarks on the Problem of Alcoholism." Address to the National Council on Alcoholism Annual Meeting, St. Regis Hotel, New York, NY, November 10, 1959. Syracuse University Libraries.

Ferri, Marica, Laura Amato, and Marina Davoli. "Alcoholics Anonymous and Other 12-Step Programmes for Alcohol Dependence." *Cochrane Database of Systematic Reviews* 3 (July 19, 2006).

———. *Alcoholics Anonymous and Other 12-Step Programs for Alcohol Dependence*. Report, Cochrane Collaboration, November 21, 2009.

Fine, Mary Jane. "Can Alcoholics Cut Back? Doc Caught in Clash of Rival Treatments." *New York Daily News*, July 16, 2000.

Finley, Steven W. "Influence of Carl Jung and William James on the Origin of Alcoholics Anonymous." *Review of General Psychology* 4, no. 1 (March 2000).

Finn, Robin. "Sudden Exit Still Stuns Addiction Expert." Public Lives, *New York Times*, July 26, 2000.

Flannery, Mary. "One Pill at a Time." *Philadelphia Daily News*, January 25, 1995.

Fox, Ruth. *Report of the Medical Director*. Internal document, National Council on Alcoholism, June 10, 1965. Syracuse University Libraries.

Franck, Johan, and Nitya Jayaram-Lindström. "Pharmacotherapy for Alcohol Dependence: Status of Current Treatments." *Current Opinion in Neurobiology* 23, no. 4 (August 2013).

Franklin, Paul. *Conclusions and Recommendations from the February 1957 Report on the National Council on Alcoholism*. National Council on Alcoholism, February 1957. Syracuse University Libraries.

Freedland, Jonathan. "New Drug Takes the Lift Out of Booze." *Guardian*, January 19, 1995.

Freedman, Judith. "Presidential Candidates: Harold Hughes." *Harvard Crimson*, March 20, 1971.

Fuller, Richard K. "Alcoholism Treatment in the United States: An Overview." *Alcohol Research & Health* 23, no. 2 (1999).

Gardner, John W. Press release and statement, US Department of Health, Education, and Welfare, October 20, 1966. LBJ Presidential Library.

———. Report to President Lyndon B. Johnson, October 11, 1966. LBJ Presidential Library.

Gardner, Yvelin. "Memorandum Re: the Driver Case." January 31, 1966. Syracuse University Libraries.

Gilbert, Douglas. Letter to Marty Mann, November 15, 1944. LBJ Presidential Library.

———. Letter to David J. Pittman, March 13, 1966. LBJ Presidential Library.

Glaser, Frederick B. "The Origins of the Drug-Free Therapeutic Community." *British Journal of Addiction* 76, no. 1 (March 1981).

Glazer, Gabrielle. "Addiction, Drunk Driving, and Suicide: The Struggles of Audrey Conn, Founder of Moderation Management." *Daily Beast*, January 11, 2015. www .thedailybeast.com/addiction-drunk-driving-and-suicide-the-struggles-of-audrey -conn-founder-of-moderation-management.

Gordis, Enoch. "FY 1999 President's Budget Request for NIAAA—Director's Statement Before the House Committee on Appropriations Subcommittee on Labor, Health and Human Services, Education and Related Agencies." NIAA, March 19, 1998. www .niaaa.nih.gov/about-niaaa/our-funding/congressional-testimony/fy-1999-presidents -budget-request-niaaa-directors.

———. "The National Institute on Alcohol Abuse and Alcoholism: Past Accomplishments and Future Goals." *Alcohol Health & Research World* 19, no. 1 (1995).

Gorman, Mike. "Summary Statement on Fiscal 1976 Budget for National Institute on Alcohol Abuse and Alcoholism." Senate Appropriations Committee on Labor-HEW, Washington, DC, June 24, 1975. National Archives, College Park, MD.

Gulick, Merle A. *President's Report*. National Council on Alcoholism, April 10, 1964. Syracuse University Libraries.

Gundersen, Gunnar. "Medicine Mobilizes Against Alcoholism." Lecture to the Annual Meeting of the National Committee on Alcoholism, Chicago, IL, March 28–29, 1957. Syracuse University Libraries.

Hagan, G. Elliott, Jr. Telephone interview by author, August 27, 2017.

Haggard, Howard W. "Critique of the Concept of the Allergic Nature of Alcohol Addiction." *Journal of Studies on Alcohol* 5 (September 1944).

———. "The Physician and the Alcoholic." *Journal of Studies on Alcohol* 7, no. 2 (1945).

Haggard, Howard W., and E. M. Jellinek. *Alcohol Explored*. New York: Doubleday, Doran & Company, 1954.

Hasin, Deborah S., Frederick S. Stinson, Elizabeth Ogburn, and Bridget F. Grant. "Prevalence, Correlates, Disability, and Comorbidity of DSM-IV Alcohol Abuse and Dependence in the United States." *Archives of General Psychiatry* 64, no. 7 (2007).

Hazelden Betty Ford Foundation. "The History of Hazelden." Official website, accessed November 20, 2018, www.hazeldenbettyford.org/about-us/history/hazelden.

Heilig, Markus. "New Treatments for Alcoholics: Twelve Steps Often Aren't Enough; Medical Breakthroughs Can Help." *Pittsburgh Post-Gazette*, December 1, 2013.

Hester, Reid K. Telephone interview by author, August 23, 2017.

Hester, Reid K., and William R. Miller. *Handbook of Alcoholism Treatment Approaches: Effective Alternatives*. Boston: Allyn and Bacon, 2003.

Hewitt, Brenda G. "The Creation of the National Institute on Alcohol Abuse and Alcoholism." *Alcohol Health & Research World* 19, no. 1 (1995).

Highway Safety Institute Public Communication Group. *Alcohol/Safety Public Information Campaigns, Seminar 1: A Report of an Informal Meeting Held May 3, 1973, to Discuss Selected Campaigns on Alcohol and Highway Safety*. Highway Safety Institute, 1973. National Archives, College Park, MD.

Hock, Ruth. Letter to Clarence Snyder, April 11, 1940. Brown University Archives.

Holmes, John Haynes. "One Year of Repeal." *Christian Century*, November 7, 1934.

———. "The Second Year of Repeal." *Christian Century*, December 4, 1935.

———. "The Third Year of Repeal." *Christian Century*, November 25, 1936.

Hood, Clifford F. Letter to President Lyndon B. Johnson, March 4, 1966. LBJ Presidential Library.

Horvath, Tom. Telephone interview by author, August 30, 2017.

Houston, Franklin. Letter to Marty Mann, October 1949. Syracuse University Libraries.

Hughes, Harold E. Letter to Marty Mann, January 18, 1972. Syracuse University Libraries.

———. Remarks to the North American Conference on Alcohol and Drug Problems, San Francisco, CA, December 13, 1974. University of Iowa Libraries.

Humphreys, Keith. "Psychotherapy and the Twelve Steps Approach for Substance Abusers: The Limits of Integration." *Psychotherapy* 30, no. 2 (1993).

Humphreys, Keith, Eric S. Mankowski, Rudolf H. Moos, and John W. Finney. "Do Enhanced Friendship Networks and Active Coping Mediate the Effect of Self-Help Groups on Substance Abuse?" *Annals of Behavioral Medicine* 21, no. 1 (1999).

Hutchison, Percy. "Alcoholic Experience." *New York Times*, June 25, 1939.

Hutt, Peter. Telephone interview by author, August 13, 2017.

Inge, William. "Max." Teleplay, 1954. Syracuse University Libraries.

Jellinek, E. M. *The Disease Concept of Alcoholism*. New Haven: College and University Press, 1960.

————. "Phases of Alcohol Addiction." *Journal of Studies on Alcohol* 13, no. 4 (1952).

————. "Recent Trends in Alcoholism and in Alcohol Consumption." *Quarterly Journal of Studies on Alcohol* 8, no. 1 (June 1947).

Jensen, Andrew. Letter to Marty Mann, April 30, 1963. Syracuse University Libraries.

Johnson, Bruce Holley. *The Alcoholism Movement in America: A Study in Cultural Innovation*. PhD diss., University of Illinois at Urbana-Champaign, 1973.

Johnson, Lyndon B. "Special Message to the Congress on Domestic Health and Education." March 1, 1966. LBJ Presidential Library.

Jones, Pat. "Drink Report Again Raises Senate Fever." *Richmond Times-Dispatch*, January 29, 1938.

Journal of Nervous and Mental Disease. Review of *Alcoholics Anonymous*. Vol. 92 (1940).

Journal of the American Medical Association. Review of *Alcoholics Anonymous*. Vol. 113, no. 16 (1939).

K., Bob. "Charles B. Towns." AA Agnostica, October 6, 2013. https://aaagnostica .org/2013/10/06/charles-b-towns/.

K., Mitchell, and Ernest Kurtz. *How It Worked: The Story of Clarence H. Snyder and the Early Days of Alcoholics Anonymous in Cleveland, Ohio*. New York: AA Big Book Study Group, 1999.

Kandel, Aben. "The Lost One." Teleplay, 1954. Syracuse University Libraries.

Kaskutas, Lee Ann. "Alcoholics Anonymous Effectiveness: Faith Meets Science." *Journal of Addictive Diseases* 28, no. 2 (2009).

Kelly, John F., Christopher W. Kahler, and Keith Humphreys. "Assessing Why Substance Use Disorder Patients Drop Out from or Refuse to Attend 12-Step Mutual-Help Groups: The 'REASONS' Questionnaire." *Addiction Research & Theory* 18, no. 3 (2010).

Kholos, Bob. "Sen. Harold Hughes—Last of the Great Democrats." *Saigonbob* (blog), 2006. https://saigonbob.typepad.com/saigonbob/2006/11/senharold_e_hug.html.

Kishline, Audrey, and Sheryl Maloy. *Face to Face: A Deadly Drunk Driver, a Grieving Young Mother, and Their Astonishing True Story of Tragedy and Forgiveness*. New York: Meredith Books, 2007.

Koob, George F. Interview by author, September 25, 2015.

————. *NIAAA Director's Report on Institute Activities to the 140th Meeting of the National Advisory Council on Alcohol Abuse and Alcoholism*. National Institute on Alcohol Abuse and Alcoholism, September 17, 2015.

————. "The Potential of Neuroscience to Inform Treatment." *Alcohol Research & Health* 33, nos. 1–2 (2010).

———. Telephone interview by author, September 30, 2014.

Kownacki, Richard J., and William R. Shadish. "Does Alcoholics Anonymous Work? The Results from a Meta-analysis of Controlled Experiments." *Substance Use & Misuse* 34, no. 13 (November 1999).

Krentzman, Amy R. "The Evidence Base for the Effectiveness of Alcoholics Anonymous: Implications for Social Work Practice." *Journal of Social Work Practice in the Addictions* 7, no. 4 (2007).

Kribben, Earl. Letter to Marty Mann, October 21, 1944. Syracuse University Libraries.

Kurtz, Ernest. *A.A.: The Story.* New York: Harper & Row, 1988.

———. *Not-God: A History of Alcoholics Anonymous.* Center City, MN: Hazelden, 1991.

L., John P. "Alcoholics Anoymous." Lecture to the Annual Meeting of the National Committee on Alcoholism, Chicago, IL, March 28–29, 1957. Syracuse University Libraries.

Latimer, James. "But What Good Came of It at Last?" *Richmond Times-Dispatch,* March 12, 1938.

———. "House Votes to See Report on Alcohol." *Richmond Times-Dispatch,* March 6, 1938.

Lattin, Don. *Distilled Spirits: Getting High, Then Sober, with a Famous Writer, a Forgotten Philosopher, and a Hopeless Drunk.* Berkeley: University of California Press, 2012.

Laundergan, J. Clark. *Easy Does It: Alcoholism Treatment Outcomes, Hazelden and the Minnesota Model.* Center City, MN: Hazelden, 1982.

Leary, Warren E. "Heroin Medication Approved as Treatment for Alcoholism." *New York Times,* January 18, 1995.

Lee, Donald B. Letter to President Lyndon B. Johnson, June 17, 1966. LBJ Presidential Library.

Leggio, Lorenzo. Interview by author, September 24, 2015.

Lewin Group. *Market Barriers to the Development of Pharmacotherapies for the Treatment of Cocaine Abuse and Addiction: Final Report.* Lewin Group, 1997.

Li, Ting-Kai. *NIAAA Director's Report on Institute Activities to 118th Advisory Council Meeting.* National Institute on Alcohol Abuse and Alcoholism, June 5, 2008. Syracuse University Libraries.

Locastro, Joseph S., Jennifer Sharpe Potter, Dennis M. Donovan, David Couper, and Kimberly W. Pope. "Characteristics of First-Time Alcohol Treatment Seekers: The COMBINE Study." *Journal of Studies on Alcohol and Drugs* 69, no. 6 (2008).

Lost Weekend. Directed by Billy Wilder. Paramount Pictures, 1945.

Lovell, Harold W. Letter to R. Brinkley Smithers, January 14, 1959. Syracuse University Libraries.

———. "Report of the President." Lecture to the Annual Meeting of the National Committee on Alcoholism, Chicago, IL, March 28–29, 1957. Syracuse University Libraries.

Low Dose Naltrexone Homepage, The. "A History of Naltrexone." Accessed November 20, 2018. www.lowdosenaltrexone.org/gazorpa/History.html.

MacLeod, Colin M. Letter to Joseph Califano Jr., February 18, 1966. LBJ Presidential Library.

Magura, Stephen, Charles M. Cleland, and J. Scott Tonigan. "Evaluating Alcoholics Anonymous's Effect on Drinking in Project MATCH Using Cross-Lagged Regression Panel Analysis." *Journal of Studies on Alcohol and Drugs* 74, no. 3 (May 2013).

Mangan, Joseph T. "The Priest Can Help." Lecture to the Annual Meeting of the National Committee on Alcoholism, Chicago, IL, March 28–29, 1957. Syracuse University Libraries.

Mann, Marty. Address to the Boston Committee on Alcoholism, October 3, 1950. Syracuse University Libraries.

———. "Alcoholics Anonymous." Address to the Economic Club of Detroit, Detroit, MI, November 25, 1946. *Vital Speeches of the Day* 13, no. 8 (February 1947).

———. Letter to all affiliates of the National Council on Alcoholism, April 16, 1959. Syracuse University Libraries.

———. Letter to Julian Armstrong, September 8, 1945. Syracuse University Libraries.

———. Letter to Katie Binyon, May 6, 1949. Syracuse University Libraries.

———. Letter to Robert H. Felix, November 4, 1959. Syracuse University Libraries.

———. Letter to Robert H. Felix, November 23, 1959. Syracuse University Libraries.

———. Letter to Don S. Fleming, February 26, 1948. Syracuse University Libraries.

———. Letter to Douglas Gilbert, November 17, 1944. Syracuse University Libraries.

———. Letter to Carl H. Gitlitz, October 18, 1947. Syracuse University Libraries.

———. Letter to Gra-Car Inc., c/o Mr. Harry B. Carroll, August 16, 1954. Syracuse University Libraries.

———. Letter to Howard Haggard, February 26, 1946. Syracuse University Libraries.

———. Letter to Howard Haggard, August 10, 1948. Syracuse University Libraries.

———. Letter to Tanis Higgins, *Reader's Digest* Research Department, January 24, 1961. Syracuse University Libraries.

———. Letter to Franklin Houston, January 30, 1949. Syracuse University Libraries.

———. Letter to Mitchel Leigh Hunt, January 4, 1963. Syracuse University Libraries.

———. Letter to President Lyndon B. Johnson, March 9, 1966. LBJ Presidential Library.

———. Letter to President Lyndon B. Johnson, March 13, 1968. LBJ Presidential Library.

———. Letter to Earl Kribben, October 24, 1944. Syracuse University Libraries.

————. Letter to John Lamont, Esq, Rinehart & Co., July 25, 1951. Syracuse University Libraries.

————. Letter to Karl Menninger, February 11, 1955. Syracuse University Libraries.

————. Letter to Karl Menninger, May 4, 1955. Syracuse University Libraries.

————. Letter to Karl Menninger, May 16, 1955. Syracuse University Libraries.

————. Letter to Karl Menninger, May 20, 1955. Syracuse University Libraries.

————. Letter to Karl Menninger, December 5, 1955. Syracuse University Libraries.

————. Letter to Merlin L. Neff, February 21, 1947. Syracuse University Libraries.

————. Letter to H. M. Page, September 23, 1954. Syracuse University Libraries.

————. Letter to H. M. Page, May 6, 1955. Syracuse University Libraries.

————. Letter to Natalie Rogers, January 21, 1947. Syracuse University Libraries.

————. Letter to Natalie Rogers, June 10, 1947. Syracuse University Libraries.

————. Letter to L. C. Twitchell, April 16, 1947. Syracuse University Libraries.

————. Letter to Mildred N. Weldon, October 11, 1948. Syracuse University Libraries.

————. Letter to Ward Wheelock ("This I Believe"), October 7, 1953. Syracuse University Libraries.

————. Letter to Walker Winslow, February 6, 1948. Syracuse University Libraries.

————. *Marty Mann Answers Your Questions About Drinking and Alcoholism.* New York: Holt, Rinehart and Winston, 1970.

————. *Marty Mann's New Primer on Alcoholism: How People Drink, How to Recognize Alcoholics, and What to Do About Them.* New York: Henry Holt, 1981.

————. "Memo on: National Committee for Education on Alcoholism." March 1944. Syracuse University Libraries.

————. "Memorandum Re: Congressional Action on District of Columbia Bill." December 20, 1967. Syracuse University Libraries.

————. "Memorandum Re: Congressional Developments." March 23, 1966. Syracuse University Libraries.

————. "Memorandum Re: Congressional Hearings on Hagan Bill." October 12, 1965. Syracuse University Libraries.

————. "Memorandum Re: Correct Use of NCA Symbol." August 22, 1961. Syracuse University Libraries.

————. "Memorandum Re: Federal Legislation on Alcoholism." February 10, 1966. Syracuse University Libraries.

————. "Memorandum Regarding Report of the Cooperative Commission on the Study of Alcoholism." October 25, 1967. Syracuse University Libraries.

————. "Minneapolis, MN" (travel report). November 10, 1960. Syracuse University Libraries.

————. Personal notes from Yale Summer School of Alcohol Studies. 1944. Syracuse University Libraries.

——. "Re: Proposed Outline of TV Series." July 2, 1954. Syracuse University Libraries.

——. *Report of the Executive Director.* National Council on Alcoholism, June 11, 1964. Syracuse University Libraries.

——. "Sarasota, FL" (travel report). May 16, 1960. Syracuse University Libraries.

——. "St. Paul Minnesota" (travel report). November 1, 1966. Syracuse University Libraries.

——. "Teamwork." Address to the Annual Meeting of the National Committee on Alcoholism, March 28–29, 1957. Syracuse University Libraries.

——. Telegram to President Lydon B. Johnson, March 13, 1968. LBJ Presidential Library.

——. "This I Believe" (draft of radio address). N.d. Syracuse University Libraries.

——. "Washington, D.C." (travel report). February 11, 1963. Syracuse University Libraries.

Margaret Arlen Program. "Interview with Marty Mann." CBS, May 20, 1949. Syracuse University Libraries.

Markel, Howard. "An Alcoholic's Savior: Was It God, Belladonna or Both?" *New York Times*, April 19, 2010.

Market, Morris. "Alcoholics and God." *Liberty*, September 1939.

Marlatt, G. Alan. "The Controlled Drinking Controversy: A Commentary." *American Psychologist* 38, no. 10 (1983).

Marlatt, G. Alan, Mary E. Larimer, John S. Baer, and Lori A. Quigley. "Harm Reduction for Alcohol Problems: Moving Beyond the Controlled Drinking Controversy." *Behavior Therapy* 24, no. 4 (Autumn 1993).

Matin, Andrew. "Rollie Hemsley: How a Hard Drinking Catcher Made Alcoholics Anonymous an International Phenomenon." Seamheads.com, April 27, 2014. http://seamheads.com/blog/2012/04/27/rollie-hemsley-how-a-hard-drinking-catcher-made-alcoholics-anonymous-an-international-phenomenon/.

Maugh, Thomas H., II. "U.S. Approves 1st New Drug to Treat Alcoholism in 47 Years." *Los Angeles Times*, January 17, 1995.

McCambridge, Mercedes. "Address to the Fourth Annual Conference on Alcoholism—NIAAA." June 24, 1974. National Archives, College Park, MD.

McCarthy, Raymond G. "A Public Clinic Approach to Certain Aspects of Alcoholism." *Journal of Studies on Alcohol* 6, no. 1 (March 1946).

McCord, William J. "Legislative Outlook for Alcoholism Care and Control, 90th Congress, 1st Session." Address to the National Council on Alcoholism Annual Meeting, Flint, MI, April 11, 1967. Syracuse University Libraries.

McCullers, Carson. Letter to Marty Mann, June 26, 1950. Syracuse University Libraries.

——. Letter to Marty Mann, June 28, 1950. Syracuse University Libraries.

———. Letter to Marty Mann, September 4, 1950. Syracuse University Libraries.

McElrath, Damian. *Hazelden: A Spiritual Odyssey.* Center City, MN: Hazelden, 1987.

———. *The Story Behind the Little Red Book: The Evolution of a Twelve Step Classic.* Center City, MN: Hazelden, 2014.

McIntire, Don. "How Well Does A.A. Work? An Analysis of Published A.A. Surveys (1968–1996)." *Alcoholism Treatment Quarterly* 18, no. 4 (2000).

Menninger, Karl. Letter to Marty Mann, February 18, 1955. Syracuse University Libraries.

———. Letter to Marty Mann, April 14, 1955. Syracuse University Libraries.

Menninger, William C. "The Billion-Dollar Hangover." Lecture to the Annual Meeting of the National Committee on Alcoholism, Chicago, IL, March 28–29, 1957. Syracuse University Libraries.

Miller, Floyd. "First Lady of Alcoholism." MS, 1960. Syracuse University Libraries.

Miller, William R. *Alcoholism: Theory, Research, and Treatment.* Lexington, MA: Ginn Press, 1992.

———. "Alcoholism American Style: A View from Abroad." *Bulletin of the Society of Psychologists in Addictive Behaviors* 2 (January 1983).

———. "Haunted by the Zeitgeist: Reflections on Contrasting Treatment Goals and Concepts of Alcoholism in Europe and the United States." *Annals of the New York Academy of Sciences* 472 (July 1986).

———. *Motivational Enhancement Therapy Manual: A Clinical Research Guide for Therapists Treating . . . Individuals with Alcohol Abuse and Dependence.* Brattleboro, VT: Echo Point Books & Media, 2014.

———. "Retire the Concept of 'Relapse.'" *Substance Use & Misuse* 50, nos. 8–9 (2015).

———. Telephone interview by author, October 25, 2017.

Miller, William, and Kathleen Carroll. *Rethinking Substance Abuse: What the Science Shows, and What We Should Do About It.* New York: Guilford Publications, 2011.

Miller, William R., and Stephen Rollnick. *Motivational Interviewing: Preparing People to Change Addictive Behavior.* New York: Guilford Press, 1995.

Miller, William R., Scott T. Walters, and Melanie E. Bennett. "How Effective Is Alcoholism Treatment in the United States?" *Journal of Studies on Alcohol* 62, no. 2 (2001).

Miller, William R., Verner S. Westerberg, Richard J. Harris, and J. Scott Tonigan. "What Predicts Relapse? Prospective Testing of Antecedent Models." *Addiction* 91 (1996).

Minetree, Harry. "Alcoholism's Sober Philanthropist." *Town and Country*, May 1986.

Mitchel, Dale. *Silkworth: The Little Doctor Who Loved Drunks.* Center City, MN: Hazelden, 2002.

Monroe, Linda Roach. "Pill Breaks Alcohol's Grip." *Chicago Tribune*, May 7, 1993.

Moos, Rudolf H., and Bernice S. Moos. "Long-Term Influence of Duration and Frequency of Participation in Alcoholics Anonymous on Individuals with Alcohol

Use Disorders." *Journal of Consulting and Clinical Psychology* 72, no. 1 (February 2004).

Moyers, Bill. "An Interview with George Koob, M.D." PBS official website, 1998. www.pbs.org/wnet/closetohome/science/html/koob.html (site discontinued).

———. "President's Statement on Domestic Health and Education, Draft." February 28, 1966. LBJ Presidential Library.

Mulford, H. A. "Measuring Public Acceptance of the Alcoholic as a Sick Person." *Quarterly Journal of Studies on Alcohol* 25, no. 1 (1964).

Murphy, Dennis. "Road to Recovery." *Dateline NBC*, September 1, 2013. Transcript via NBC News official website, www.nbcnews.com/id/14627442/ns/dateline_nbc/t /road-recovery/.

My Name Is Bill W. Hallmark Hall of Fame, CBS, April 30, 1989.

National Committee for Education on Alcoholism. *Annual Report*. NCEA, 1945. Syracuse University Libraries.

———. *Annual Report*. NCEA, 1946. Syracuse University Libraries.

———. *Annual Report*. NCEA, 1947. Syracuse University Libraries.

———. *Annual Report*. NCEA, 1948. Syracuse University Libraries.

———. *Annual Report*. NCEA, 1949. Syracuse University Libraries.

———. "Confidential 'Blue-Print' for Early Committee Organizers." N.d. Syracuse University Libraries.

———. *5-Year Plan*. NCEA, 1949. Syracuse University Libraries.

———. "Instructions for Sending Out Publicity for Mrs. Mann." March 15, 1948. Syracuse University Libraries.

———. "Possibilities for the National Committee." 1945. Syracuse University Libraries.

———. "Special Bulletin." December 28, 1949. Syracuse University Libraries.

National Committee on Alcoholism. *1956 Objectives*. National Committee on Alcoholism, 1956. Syracuse University Libraries.

———. Transcript of the Annual Meeting of the National Committee on Alcoholism, Chicago, IL, March 28–29, 1957. Syracuse University Libraries.

———. Transcript of meeting of the National Committee on Alcoholism Institute for Hospital Administrators, Statler Hotel, New York, NY, March 31, 1956. Syracuse University Libraries.

National Council on Alcoholism. Comment, January 11, 1971. Syracuse University Libraries.

———. Comment, May 27, 1971. Syracuse University Libraries.

———. Comment, December 15, 1971. Syracuse University Libraries.

———. Comment, May 15, 1974. Syracuse University Libraries.

———. Comment, June 18, 1975. Syracuse University Libraries.

——. Comment, July 17, 1975. Syracuse University Libraries.

——. "Fifteenth Anniversary Dinner Bulletin." October 1, 1959. Syracuse University Libraries.

——. "Memorandum Re: Arthur Cain Article in *Saturday Evening Post.*" October 1964. Syracuse University Libraries.

——. Minutes of board of directors meeting, January 14, 1958. Syracuse University Libraries.

——. Minutes of the 1963 National Council on Alcoholism Annual Meeting, April 18–19, 1963. Syracuse University Libraries.

——. *NCA Newsletter*, Winter 1967–68. Syracuse University Libraries.

——. "Notes on the Franklin Report." N.d. Syracuse University Libraries.

——. *Publicity Handbook for NCA Affiliates.* NCA, 1958. Syracuse University Libraries.

——. "Summary Statement, Application for NIAAA Grant." June 1976. National Archives, College Park, MD.

National Institute on Alcohol Abuse and Alcoholism. Minutes of the 27th Meeting of the National Advisory Council on Alcohol Abuse and Alcoholism, March 21–22, 1978. Syracuse University Libraries.

——. "Naltrexone Approved for Alcoholism Treatment." January 17, 1995. www.niaaa .nih.gov/news-events/news-releases/naltrexone-approved-alcoholism-treatment.

——. "NIAAA's Clinical Investigations Group (NCIG): Making Medications Development for AUD More Efficient." N.d. Syracuse University Libraries.

——. "Projects & Initiatives." N.d. Syracuse University Libraries.

——. *Report of the National Institute on Alcohol Abuse and Alcoholism Task Force on Grants and Contracts to National Agencies Review.* NIAAA, December 1, 1976. Syracuse University Libraries.

——. *Strategic Plan 2017–2021.* NIAAA, 2017. Syracuse University Libraries.

——. Transcript of meeting of National Institute on Alcohol Abuse and Alcoholism Advisory Council, June 7–8, 1971. National Archives, College Park, MD.

——. Transcript of meeting of National Institute on Alcohol Abuse and Alcoholism Advisory Council, September 9, 1971. National Archives, College Park, MD.

——. Transcript of meeting of National Institute on Alcohol Abuse and Alcoholism Advisory Council, June 5, 1972. National Archives, College Park, MD.

——. Transcript of meeting of National Institute on Alcohol Abuse and Alcoholism Advisory Council, June 6, 1972. National Archives, College Park, MD.

——. Transcript of meeting of National Institute on Alcohol Abuse and Alcoholism Advisory Council, September 21, 1972. National Archives, College Park, MD.

——. Transcript of meeting of National Institute on Alcohol Abuse and Alcoholism Advisory Council, June 18, 1973. National Archives, College Park, MD.

———. Transcript of meeting of National Institute on Alcohol Abuse and Alcoholism Advisory Council, March 17, 1975. National Archives, College Park, MD.

———. Transcript of meeting of National Institute on Alcohol Abuse and Alcoholism Advisory Council, May 3, 1975. National Archives, College Park, MD.

———. "Treatment for Alcohol Problems: Finding and Getting Help." N.d. Syracuse University Libraries.

Nevesi, Dennis. "G. A. Marlatt, Advocate of Shift in Treating Addicts, Dies at 69." *New York Times*, March 21, 2011.

New York Times. "Alcohol Again." October 4, 1938.

———. "Scientists Launch Unbiased Study of Drink Problem." October 3, 1938.

Newsweek. "Yale University's First School of Alcohol Studies." August 23, 1943.

O'Connor, Anahad. "Drugs to Aid Alcoholics See Little Use, Study Finds." *New York Times*, May 13, 2014.

Olson, Nancy. *With a Lot of Help from Our Friends: The Politics of Alcoholism*. Bloomington, IN: Writers Club Press, 2003.

P., Bob. "A.A. and the Media." Chapter 13 of "Manuscript of A.A. World History." Unpublished MS, 1985. Via Silkworth.net, http://silkworth.net/bobp/chapter13 .html.

Pendery, M. L., and I. M. Maltzman. "Controlled Drinking by Alcoholics? New Findings and Reevaluation of a Major Affirmative Study." *Science* 217 (1982).

Pettineti, Helen M., and Margaret E. Mattson. *Medical Management Treatment Manual: A Clinical Guide for Researchers and Clinicians Providing Pharmacotherapy for Alcohol Dependence (Generic Version)*. National Institute on Alcohol Abuse and Alcoholism, 2010.

Pike, Katherine. Letter to John Deering, September 9, 1975. National Archives, College Park, MD.

———. Letter to Earnest Noble, February 3, 1974. National Archives, College Park, MD.

Pike, Thomas P. Letter to J. Paul Austin, June 25, 1976. Brown University Archives.

———. Letter to Donald B. Rice, April 21, 1975. Brown University Archives.

———. Letter to Donald B. Rice, September 10, 1975. Brown University Archives.

———. *Memoirs of Thomas P. Pike*. Pasadena, CA: Grant Dahlstrom, 1979.

Pittman, Bill. *AA: The Way It Began*. Seattle: Glen Abbey Books, 1988.

Plaut, Thomas F. A. *Alcohol Problems: A Report to the Nation by the Cooperative Commission on the Study of Alcoholism*. Oxford: Oxford University Press, 1968.

Porter, A. "Wet and Dry School." *Collier's*, October 30, 1943.

Powell v. Texas. US Supreme Court, June 17, 1968.

Quarterly Journal of Studies on Alcohol. "Activities of the Research Council." Vol. 2, no. 3 (1941).

Reeves, Richard. *President Nixon: Alone in the White House.* New York: Simon & Schuster, 2001.

Research Council on Problems of Alcohol. "Report of the Second Annual Meeting of the Research Council on Problems of Alcohol." *Quarterly Journal of Studies on Alcohol* 1, no. 1 (June 1940).

———. "Report on Research Council Activities." *Quarterly Journal of Studies on Alcohol* 4, no. 1 (June 1943).

———. "Research Council Activities." *Quarterly Journal of Studies on Alcohol* 1, no. 3 (December 1940).

———. "The Research Council on Problems of Alcohol: An Outline of Its Program, Objectives, Resources and Progress to Date." *Quarterly Journal of Studies on Alcohol* 2 (1941).

Richeson, Forrest. *Courage to Change: Beginnings, Growth and Influence of Alcoholics Anonymous in Minnesota.* Minnesota: M & M Printing, 1978.

Richmond News Leader. "A Brief for Temperance." November 7, 1938.

Richmond Times-Dispatch. "Demon Rum Dehorned in Textbook." December 28, 1937.

———. "Senate Votes to Destroy Alcohol Book." March 1, 1938.

Roizen, Ron. "The American Discovery of Alcoholism, 1933–1939." PhD diss., University of California, Berkeley, 1991.

———. "Cherry-Picking the History of the Alcoholism Movement." *Points: The Blog of the Alcohol & Drugs History Society*, May 20, 2011. https://pointsadhsblog.word press.com/2011/05/20/cherry-picking-the-history-of-the-alcoholism-movement-1/.

———. "E.M. Jellinek and All That." Roizen.com, 2000. www.roizen.com/ron/jellinek-pres.htm.

———. "E.M. Jellinek's Departure from Budapest in 1920." *Points: The Blog of the Alcohol & Drugs History Society*, August 5, 2011. https://pointsadhsblog.wordpress .com/2011/08/05/e-m-jellineks-departure-from-budapest-in-1920-part-two/.

———. "Four Unsung Moments in the Genesis of the Modern Alcoholism Movement in the United States." Unpublished MS, 1996. www.roizen.com/ron/fourunsung.html.

———. "The Great Controlled-Drinking Controversy." In *Recent Developments in Alcoholism*, vol. 5, edited by Marc Galanter. New York: Plenum, 1987.

———. "Norman Jolliffe, the Rockefeller Foundation, and the Origins of the Modern Alcoholism Movement." *Journal of Studies on Alcohol* 55, no. 4 (July 1994).

———. "Paradigm Sidetracked: Explaining Early Resistance to the Alcoholism Paradigm at Yale's Laboratory of Applied Physiology, 1940–1944." Reading at the Alcohol & Temperance History Group's International Congress on the Social History of Alcohol, London, Ontario, May 1993. www.roizen.com/ron/sidetracked.htm.

———. "What Time Do You Want It to Be? Finessing Science at the National Council on Alcoholism and at Yale." *Points: The Blog of the Alcohol & Drugs History Society.*

May 26, 2011. https://pointsadhsblog.wordpress.com/2011/05/26/what-time-do -you-want-it-to-be-finessing-science-at-the-national-council-on-alcoholism-and -at-yale/.

———. "Where Did Mrs. Marty Mann Learn Alcoholism Was a Disease and Why Should It Matter?" *Ranes Report* 7 (1997). www.roizen.com/ron/rr7.htm.

Room, Robin. "Governing Images of Alcohol and Drug Problems: The Structure, Sources, and Sequels of Conceptualizations of Intractable Problems." PhD diss., University of California, Berkeley, 1978.

Ross, Joseph S. "The Committee on the Costs of Medical Care and the History of Health Insurance in the United States." *Einstein Quarterly* 19 (2002).

Rush, Benjamin. *The Effects of Ardent Spirits upon Man.* New York: Cornelius Davis, 1811.

Rutgers Center of Alcohol Studies. "The History of the Center of Alcohol Studies." Official website, accessed November 20, 2018. https://alcoholstudies.rutgers.edu /history.

S., Arthur, Tom E., and Glenn C. *Alcoholics Anonymous (AA) Recovery Rates.* Self-published, January 1, 2008.

Sakson, Steve. "New Drug for Alcoholism." *Pittsburgh Post-Gazette*, January 18, 1995.

Salim, Onaje. Telephone interview by author, February 20, 2016.

Scholastic. "Four Years of Repeal." December 4, 1937.

Scientific Temperance Journal. "Reviews of Alcoholics Anonymous: The Story of How More Than One Hundred Men Have Recovered from Alcoholism and Alcohol in Moderation and Excess." Vol. 47 (1939).

Scott, Neil. "R. Brinkley Smithers: 35 Years of Leadership." *Alcoholism and Addictions Magazine*, October 1988.

Shoe, Thomas D. Letter to Marty Mann, January 7, 1972. Syracuse University Libraries.

Siegel, Carlton J. Letter to President Lyndon B. Johnson, September 10, 1966. LBJ Presidential Library.

Silkworth, William D. "Alcoholism as a Manifestation of Allergy." *Medical Record*, March 17, 1937.

SMART Recovery. *SMART Recovery.* 3rd ed. Mentor, OH: SMART Recovery, 2013.

Smash-Up: The Story of a Woman. Directed by Stuart Heisler. Universal Pictures, 1947.

Smith Wise, Ida B. "All Around the Mulberry Bush Again." *Union Signal*, October 15, 1938.

Smithers, R. Brinkley. Letter to President Lyndon B. Johnson, March 29, 1966. LBJ Presidential Library.

———. "Report of the Treasurer." Address to the Annual Meeting of the National Committee on Alcoholism, Chicago, IL, March 28–29, 1957. Syracuse University Libraries.

Snyder, Clarence. Letter to "Roger," March 3, 1979. Brown University Archives.

Sobell, Mark. Telephone interview by author, September 22, 2017.

Sobell, Mark B., and Linda C. Sobell. "The Aftermath of Heresy: A Response to Pendery et al.'s Critique of 'Individualized Behavior Therapy for Alcoholics.'" *Behaviour Research and Therapy* 22 (1984).

———. "Alcoholics Treated by Individualized Behavior Therapy: One Year Treatment Outcome." *Behaviour Research and Therapy* 11, no. 4 (1973).

———. "Controlled Drinking after 25 Years: How Important Was the Great Debate?" *Addiction* 90, no. 9 (September 1995).

———. "It Is Time for Low-Risk Drinking Goals to Come Out of the Closet." *Addiction* 106, no. 10 (October 2011).

———. "Moratorium on Maltzman: An Appeal to Reason." *Journal of Studies on Alcohol* 50, no. 5 (September 1989).

———. "Obstacles to the Adoption of Low Risk Drinking Goals in the Treatment of Alcohol Problems in the United States: A Commentary." *Addiction Research & Theory* 14, no. 1 (2006).

———. "Second Year Treatment Outcome of Alcoholics Treated by Individualized Behavior Therapy: Results." *Behaviour Research and Therapy* 14, no. 3 (1976).

Spicer, Jerry. *The Minnesota Model: The Evolution of the Multidisciplinary Approach to Addiction Recovery.* Center City, MN: Hazelden, 1993.

Steinhauer, Jennifer. "Addiction Center's Director Quits in Treatment Debate." *New York Times*, July 11, 2000.

Stewart, William H. Letter to Carlton J. Siegel, October 10, 1966. LBJ Presidential Library.

Suzukamo, Leslie Brooks. "MM: A New Path to Sobriety." *Saint Paul Pioneer Press*, February 3, 1998.

Thomsen, Robert. *Bill W.* Center City, MN: Hazelden, 1999.

Tiebout, Harry M. "The Syndrome of Alcohol Addiction." Lecture to Symposium on Prevention and Treatment of Alcoholism, Cleveland, OH, September 24, 1944.

———. "Therapeutic Mechanisms of Alcoholics Anonymous." *American Journal of Psychiatry* 100 (1944).

Tieman, John Samuel. "The Origins of Twelve-Step Spirituality: Bill W. and Edward Dowling, S.J." *U.S. Catholic Historian* 13, no. 3 (1995).

Timko, C., R. H. Moos, J. W. Finney, and M. D. Lesar. "Long-Term Outcomes of Alcohol Use Disorders: Comparing Untreated Individuals with Those in Alcoholics Anonymous and Formal Treatment." *Journal of Studies on Alcohol* 61, no. 4 (2000).

Tonigan, J. S., R. Toscova, and W. R. Miller. "Meta-analysis of the Literature on Alcoholics Anonymous: Sample and Study Characteristics Moderate Findings." *Journal of Studies on Alcohol* 57, no. 1 (1996).

Tournier, R. E. "Alcoholics Anonymous as Treatment and as Ideology." *Journal of Studies on Alcohol* 40, no. 3 (1979).

Trimmer, J. Maurice. "Science and the Liquor Question." *Christian Century*, January 4, 1939.

Vannicelli, Marsha. Telephone interview by author, August 12, 2017.

Verhovek, Sam Howe. "Advocate of Moderation for Heavy Drinkers Learns Sobering Lesson." *New York Times*, July 6, 2000.

Vonnegut, Kurt. *Slaughterhouse-Five*. New York: Dell, 1974.

W., Bill. *See* Wilson, Bill.

Walker, Regina. "Remembering Audrey Kishline, the Founder of Moderation Management." *Fix*, January 7, 2015.

Warne, Robet. "Remembering Former Kemper Chairman, CEO James S. Kemper, Jr." Adjustercom.com, July 8, 2002. www.adjustercom.com/modules.php?mop=mod load&name=News&func=article_view&adj_article_id=361.

Warren, Kenneth R. "NIAAA: Advancing Alcohol Research for 40 Years." *Alcohol Research & Health* 33, nos. 1–2 (2010).

———. "NIAAA Director's Report on Institute Activities to the 127th Meeting of the National Advisory Council on Alcohol Abuse and Alcoholism." NIAAA, June 9, 2011.

———. Telephone interview by author, December 18, 2015.

Westberg, Granger E. "The Pastor and the Alcoholic." Address to the Annual Meeting of the National Committee on Alcoholism, Chicago, IL, March 28–29, 1957. Syracuse University Libraries.

White, Lee C. Memorandum to Mr. F. Robert Meier, Assistant Secretary, Department of Health, Education, and Welfare, December 3, 1964. LBJ Presidential Library.

White, William L. "Addiction as a Disease: The Birth of a Concept." *Counselor* 1, no. 1 (2000).

———. "Addiction Disease Concept: Advocates and Critics." *Counselor* 2, no. 1 (2001).

———. "The Addiction-Disease Concept: Its Rise and Fall in the 19th Century." *Counselor* 1, no. 2 (2000).

———. "From Calling to Career: The Birth of Addiction Counseling as a Specialized Role." *Counselor* 17, no. 6 (1999).

———. "The History of SMART Recovery" Interview with Joe Gernstein, MD, 2012. William White Papers.

———. "The Psychology of Addiction Recovery" Interview with William R. Miller, January 2012. William White Papers.

———. "The Rebirth of the Disease Concept of Alcoholism in the 20th Century." *Counselor* 1, no. 2 (2000).

———. *Recovery/Remission from Substance Use Disorders: An Analysis of Reported Outcomes in 415 Scientific Reports, 1868–2011*. Philadelphia Department of Behavioral Health and Intellectual DisAbility Services & Great Lakes Addiction Technology Transfer Center, 2012.

———. "Reflections on the History of Alcoholics Anonymous." Interview with Ernie Kurtz, 2009. William White Papers.

———. *Slaying the Dragon: The History of Addiction Treatment and Recovery in America*. Bloomington, IL: Chestnut Health Systems, 2014.

———. "SMART Recovery." Interview with Tom Litwicki, 2013. William White Papers.

White, William L., and Ernest Kurtz. "A Message of Tolerance and Celebration: The Portrayal of Multiple Pathways of Recovery in the Writings of Alcoholics Anonymous Co-founder Bill Wilson." 2010. William White Papers.

Wiener, Carolyn L. *The Politics of Alcoholism: Building an Arena Around a Social Problem*. Piscataway, NJ: Transaction Books, 1981.

Willenbring, Mark L. "The Past and Future of Research on Treatment of Alcohol Dependence." *Alcohol Research & Health* 33, nos. 1–2 (2010).

Wilson, Bill. *Alcoholics Anonymous Comes of Age*. New York: Harper, 1957.

———. *The Language of the Heart: Bill W.'s Grapevine Writings*. New York: AA Grapevine, 1988.

———. "Let's Be Friendly with Our Friends: Friends on the Alcoholism Front." *A.A. Grapevine*, March 1958.

Wilson, Lois. *Lois Remembers: Memoirs of the Co-founder of Al-Anon and Wife of the Co-founder of Alcoholics Anonymous*. New York: Al-Anon Family Group Headquarters, 1998.

Woolf, S. J. "The Sick Person We Call an Alcoholic." *New York Times Magazine*, April 21, 1946.

Yale University. *Alcohol, Science and Society: Twenty-Nine Lectures with Discussions as Given at the Yale Summer School of Alcohol Studies*. New Haven: Yale University, Laboratory of Applied Physiology, School of Alcohol Studies, 1945.

———. *Schedule of the 1948 Yale Summer School of Alcohol Studies*. Yale University, 1948. Syracuse University Libraries.

INDEX